MAKE
MONEY
MOVE

MAKE MONEY MOVE

*A Guide to
Financial Wellness*

LAUREN SIMMONS

AMISTAD

An Imprint of HarperCollinsPublishers

HarperCollins books may be purchased for educational, business, or sales promotional use. For information, please email the Special Markets Department at SPsales@harpercollins.com.

FIRST EDITION

Designed by Ad Librum

Library of Congress Cataloging-in-Publication Data has been applied for.

ISBN 978-0-06-324653-9

23 24 25 26 27 LBC 6 5 4 3 2

I dedicate this book to my twin brother. My brother motivates me. He's the reason why I have this fire. I look at him and I have no excuses. I have this burn—he's the reason that I'm doing this. If you don't have a motivation, it is really hard to achieve and manifest any goals, whether you're working out or writing music, whether you're an actor, or a dancer, or an entrepreneur. If you don't have something that makes you want to get up every day and achieve, something that motivates you, then I wish for you that love, that spark, that joy. I hope you will feel the love that I have for my twin.

Contents

Introduction

On March 7, 2017, at just twenty-two years old, I arrived on the trading floor of the New York Stock Exchange—the day *Fearless Girl*, the now-iconic bronze sculpture by Kristen Visbal, was installed on Broad Street across from the NYSE building. Little did I know I would go on to shatter the proverbial glass ceiling by being the youngest trader ever at the New York Stock Exchange and only full-time female equity trader at the Exchange.

I was working for Rosenblatt Securities as the "Wolfette of Wall Street," which was how *Harper's Bazaar* warmly described me. I was also just the second African American woman equity trader in NYSE history to sport that prestigious badge.

Nothing about my early history would have suggested this path. I grew up in Marietta, Georgia, a suburb of Atlanta. I come from a small family consisting of my twin brother, Lawrence (Diesel), and my younger sister, Leila. We were raised in a single-parent household.

In many traditions around the world, from China to West

Africa, twins are believed to be good luck and are said to bring fortune to the family. While we didn't grow up wealthy in the material sense of the word, my twin brother and I both brought blessings to our family in unexpected ways.

My mother made sure that we had the basics. She purchased our home when I wasn't even a year old. She made it a priority for her kids to be raised in a house versus an apartment. She was very disciplined with money. Watching her make her money move would serve me later in life.

I learned how to live beneath my means and to save a majority of my income. My mother raised us on a single salary, and while she was fortunate enough to make $60,000 a year, her salary had to feed a family of four, including one with special needs whose medical bills were continuous, and so she became great at budgeting. My mother managed to save half of what she made so that we had enough to travel and could afford the occasional splurge on extras such as Xboxes.

I was the kind of kid who paid close attention to what the adults did with their money. I had some good examples in my grandparents, who were entrepreneurs. My grandfather owned his own trucking company, and my grandma is a realtor. And then there was my aunt. She lived such a fabulous life. Designer clothes, cars, handbags, a beautiful home. Looking back, I realized that just because you appear to have things doesn't mean you aren't struggling.

In suburban Georgia where I grew up, it wasn't uncommon for athletic young men to get recruited by top colleges. They were on the path to enviable multimillion-dollar sports contracts. I used to wish that I was a boy (as ridiculous as that sounds) so that I could have accessibility to making a lot of money. I didn't know how or when, but I never doubted that one day I would be wealthy.

My brother was diagnosed early on with cerebral palsy and ectodermal dysplasia. He's always been very nonchalant about his disability, very matter of fact. Diesel has this larger-than-life personality, and he just doesn't really let too many things bring him down. He's the most vocal person I know—his head is held high. He's optimistic. Growing up, I don't think I understood where he got his strength.

But in my early twenties, I was able to surrender and see the world through my brother's optimistic lens. Identifying with his point of view on life, I felt I could achieve everything and anything. I wanted to lean into life the way Diesel does. A light bulb went off.

I want you to know that even in your darkest moments you can find the light within. And beyond finances, you can also ask yourself: *What is going to be the fire that lights me day to day?*

For me, it's 100 percent my twin brother.

Because Diesel's optimism against the greatest odds touched off that light in me, I was the first member of my family to graduate from college. And the day I graduated from Kennesaw

State University with a bachelor's degree in genetics and a minor in statistics in late December 2016, I hopped on a plane to New York to start anew. I was wide open to opportunities that weren't related to my genetics degree.

We only have one life to live—why not pursue something you really love?

My first decision was to live with my grandparents in New Jersey. Being completely honest with you now, at the time I thought it was definitely not "sexy" to be an adult living with grandparents or parents. Today I say, if there's a family member you trust who you can live with, put your pride aside and use this safety net for a while to get ahead.

I felt that New York, with all of its limitless possibilities and opportunities, was a great place to start. NYC people are wonderfully transparent. Personally, I like the honesty and directness. You don't have to question what people are thinking. I would tell recruiters that I wanted to make six figures. And they would say I was overly ambitious, that earning six figures was unlikely just starting out. But it wasn't unattainable. I learned later *it wasn't ambitious enough.*

I don't believe in luck, but I do believe in being in alignment with events happening the way they should work out. After hard-core networking for three months in New York, I faced a ton of closed doors. It was exhausting emotionally, but just as I was about to break, a door opened, leading to Richard Rosenblatt, CEO of Rosenblatt Securities. I truly do believe that everything that happens, whether it's good or bad, happens exactly when we need it. And so, that being said, I didn't seek out the New York Stock Exchange. I didn't seek out a job in finance. I was just a recent grad who was open to anything.

I landed a position with Rosenblatt as an equity trader. I loved the job, but to keep it I had to pass the series 19 exam, an in-house New York Stock Exchange exam that is notoriously brutal. The test was not a joke! It was well known that out of five people taking the test, four would fail. I mean, all I did for a month was just study for this exam. I needed to prove to myself that I could do it.

My mother had very transparent conversations with me as a kid. She wanted me to have a real understanding about the way things work. My mother never allowed us to have a victim mentality. "There are always solutions to every problem," she'd say. And even now that I'm an adult, and even when I feel like there are no solutions, I'm like, Okay, well then, there must be something bigger! So you learn that you have to just kind of move forward . . . let it go and whatever is meant to be will be. I think my mother became that way because she had to care for a son with disabilities. She had to look at life like, *Okay . . . but you* can *keep moving. You* can *keep that drive. You* can *keep pushing forward.* And she didn't want my brother and me to feel like there was ever a dead end. She instilled that in us more than anything.

I passed the series 19 on my first try and gained an official position as an equity trader for Rosenblatt Securities at the New York Stock Exchange. I stood on the floor of the Exchange, knowing that I belonged there just as much as anyone else. I never saw my being an African American woman, the lone "Wolfette" in the room with 250 white guys (the two Black guys, Aaron and Tommy, were my lifelines and still are to this day), as a disadvantage. I didn't see my race and gender as barriers or deficits. Instead, *I knew these were my strengths.*

The New York Stock Exchange was not the first time in my life I'd been the "only" or the "other" in the room. In high school I was the only female in my architectural engineering class for four years, and in college I was either an "only" or one of "the very few" in genetics. In these moments, I learned to focus on my goals and stand in my strength. I wasn't going to allow others to make me feel as though I wasn't supposed to be there. I believe that life gives us these moments, like pieces to a larger puzzle, to help prepare us for the next moments in our lives.

The second day I was on the floor of the Exchange, I was told: "Pretty women don't wind up staying on the floor, they end up going into, like, PR or something." I was like, "okay . . . noted." While I didn't even see myself at the time as "pretty" (I still had a lot of inner work to do), I was driven to prove them wrong. Some people call it ambition, but it's really all about an abundance mindset. When you're just like, *There's room for me, there's a path for me.*

Ultimately the men on the floor of the New York Stock Exchange showed me that we as people are more the same than not. We may be culturally or racially or physically different. We may come from different levels of privilege and access in society, but at the end of the day most of us want the same things.

During my two years on the trading floor, I learned how to take calculated risks and how to work in a male-dominated environment. I learned budgeting and saving and got better at managing my finances while making only $12,000 a year. I learned that it was okay that I hadn't invested one dime in the stock market. It turns out that most men on the floor don't play in the market. During my time at the NYSE, I worked with institutional clients, meaning people with a net worth of over $1 million. Eventually I left the floor and decided to not go into another traditional finance job for two reasons: (1) because of what my story represents, and (2) because I was told directly that I couldn't continue growing my brand and be an employee of a firm.

It wasn't until I left the floor that I found my passion. I am called to educate and demystify personal finance, particularly for those who are being left out in the dark when it comes to mind, body, money—millennials, Gen Zers, women, minorities, and honestly anybody on the outside looking in.

There have been so many books written by successful older men about career success, business, and investing. While many are helpful and inspiring, people who feel like "the other" can find them difficult to relate to; the promises of success in these books feel out of reach and unachievable for people who don't look like the authors or come from similar backgrounds. It's much easier to attempt to follow in the footsteps of someone who looks like you or comes from similar circumstances.

As of 2023, there are only fifty-three female CEOs of Fortune 500 companies. That is only 10 percent. Minority women account for less than 4 percent of roles in finance. There needs to be more overall diversity on Wall Street, and I don't just mean through hiring practices but in clients as well.

One of the most important lessons that I learned from my experience at the Exchange is that money is very practical. It relies on simple math—straightforward concepts such as addition and subtraction. Even if you're not so great at math, you can attain money. You can understand it.

You can do it.

My family and I have come a long way. I'm on my way to achieving million-dollar dreams, and I believe that, using the concepts presented in this book, you can do it too! It's all about mind, body, money. So let's go make some money move. I'll show you how.

Financial Wellness

Financial wellness means freedom for your body and freedom for your mind. Financial wellness can have a positive effect on your entire life, not only when it comes to money and finances, but when it comes to the quality and ease of *how* you live. Financial stress can wreak all kinds of havoc on your overall wellness. If you're stressed about money, you can make yourself physically ill as the mental stress leads to physical stress, which can lead to sickness. Financial stress can also cause the breakdown of your relationships with your family, friends, or partner. All of these impacts of financial stress can absolutely lead to the deterioration of your overall quality of life.

According to a 2021 Capital One CreditWise survey, 73 percent of Americans ranked their finances as the number one cause of stress in their lives. That's most people living in this country!

So ask yourself this important question: *What is my relationship with money?*

No one else is going to answer that question for you.

Bad relationships with money don't discriminate. It doesn't matter if you're rich or poor. It is well known that NBA players can get contracts worth upward of $45 million per year. By definition, it would seem like they have financial wellness, yet so many players go bankrupt after they retire. They literally have $0 in their account! Hard to wrap your head around, right? According to *Sports Illustrated*, within five years of leaving the NBA, 60 percent of former NBA players are broke. So financial wellness is more than just a matter of money.

You can be given a winning lottery ticket today, but does that mean you're going to stay wealthy? Are you going to be happy? Does coming into money mean that you will have better spending, investing, and saving habits? Does being rich mean that you're growing? Does it mean that you know what *to do* with your money? No. And so you see, the quality of the relationships between ourselves, our money, and our minds and bodies is hugely correlated. Everything we consume both physically and mentally, even right down to the quality of sleep that we get each day, is interconnected and directly—sometimes drastically—affects how we navigate through our day-to-day lives. All of our issues are interconnected.

They're all important.

I first understood these interconnections when I began working on my mind. I was starting to build a positive mindset, instead of walking around just being so angry at the world and my life circumstances.

It's harder to be angry than it is to just feel good. It's not that it's easier to do the work but it feels better to feel good than it does to be pissed off at the world. Would you rather feel light and airy and free or be in a vibrationally negative space?

When I changed my perspective, I was able to begin to envision different circumstances for myself, a different world for myself, a different way of being. I started to see a clearer picture of myself, one surrounded by wellness, by wealth, by money. But it was also really easy to see the money part quickly, not because I was bad with money, but because money is an energy thing. Money can come, and it can just as easily go. You will find that it's here, and then it's not.

Cultivating financial wellness takes time and practice and inner work.

I was making only $12,000 a year when I first began working at the New York Stock Exchange, and I can't tell you how absolutely happy I was, how free I felt. I was enjoying my life every day. I was learning, and I was growing. When I started making real money—over six figures—and could suddenly travel and have access to what I wanted and build my future, I realized that my life wasn't so different. Some people might find that jarring, asking, "How is that possible?"

It was possible because I continued being grateful for small things, being present, journaling, meditating. I changed none of my rituals. I vibrationally was in the same space even if my outer world at the time didn't reflect my inner world. I also had a gut feeling, an ultimate knowing. In the definitive way that you know your name is [fill in the blank], I knew that I'd make money and that my outer world would someday be a reflection of how I felt internally.

I was grateful to just be in New York City. I felt rich just looking at the taxis going by, just going to the park and enjoying nature. *True value, true wealth, comes from knowing the value of your journey. It comes from building a great relationship with yourself—one of the most important practices that you can ever work on.* How you show up for yourself dictates how you show up in this world. What is your purpose? What is your passion? What is going to drive you? Beyond that, showing up for yourself dictates the value that you put on money and shapes your relationship with money.

Remember, this isn't a sprint, it's a marathon.
You can't try to jump ahead and take shortcuts.
It's going to happen exactly the way that it's meant to.
So what you can do in the process is just enjoy life!
Just enjoy being, just enjoy being grateful.

Journaling

Words have power. Putting pen to paper has power. *You really want to be intentional about what you're writing down, and intentional about what you speak out loud.* Using negative words, saying things like "I'm so stupid" or "I'm bad" or "I'm never going to be good with money" can give you just that. Do you want to sabotage your financial wellness?

I'm constantly hearing people say, "I don't know anything about money," or "I'm so bad at money, like, I can never make good money." *Let's change that narrative.* To be intentional is to have an honest conversation with yourself. A good place to start is journaling.

Do a Self-Audit

Take stock of your relationship with money and also be gentle with yourself. If you aren't good with money, did you ever think that maybe there's a reason why? Our relationship with money is a reflection of the community around us. If our parents are bad with money, we have the power to decide if we will be like our parents or if we'll be the opposite. Could it be that you *believe* that you're bad at money? Are you bad at managing your money because you weren't so great at math when you were a kid? Maybe your parents never talked to you about money?

Grab a pen and paper, or even the notes app on your phone, and get ready to answer some questions:

▸ What would you like to say to your younger self about money?

▸ What do you believe about yourself when it comes to money?

▸ What was your parents' relationship with money?

▸ What words did they use when speaking about money? How did that make you feel?

▸ Were there any good examples of using money well around you growing up?

▸ Do you openly talk about money with friends or family?

▸ What do you believe about money?

▸ Are you good with money?

▸ How do you feel about your current financial situation?

‣ What would you like to change about your finances?

‣ What would you like to change about your life?

Be willing to own up to being bad with money in order to be good with money.

If you're bad with money, then let's immediately create a new affirmation. Get in front of a mirror and say it loud: "I intend to have a healthy relationship with money!" We have set the intention. Many of us, especially women, are taught that talking about money is taboo. *We must be willing to talk about money.*

Self-Reflection

I learned about "mirror work" from motivational author Louise Hay and her book *Mirror Work*. Hay talks about standing in front of the mirror to have a conversation with yourself and really making eye contact with the person in the mirror. You can talk to your younger self, or even your future self. It's important to feel what you're saying. This kind of work is so relevant today because millennials and Gen Zers spend so much time virtually and don't always make eye contact with other people. I have a few favorite affirmations that I say every single day while talking to myself in the mirror:

"I love my life."

"I'm grateful for my life."

"Abundance." (*repeated five times*)

Get to Know Yourself

I had to learn how to look at myself—I mean really look at myself—in the mirror. The first few times I would find myself bawling in tears because, until then, I'd been saying affirmations, but I didn't truly feel them until I actually *looked* myself in the eyes.

My mom would tell me: "You're smart, you're good at basketball, you're beautiful." But before I'd come to believe it myself, it was just white noise. I always assumed that that is just what parents say to their kids, and maybe it is, but it's how we choose to receive the message. Do we want to believe that we're beautiful, smart, and successful? We have to choose to receive the message or not; we always have the power to accept positivity or negativity, it's our choice. It's often easier for us to receive a negative comment than it is for us to receive a positive one.

There's a moment when we really begin to internalize something that is repeated to us consistently. If you hear it enough, you're going to believe it.

Take a look at yourself in the mirror, hold your gaze for an entire minute, and then try to answer these questions aloud, and honestly:

What are five things that you love about yourself?

What are five things that you're proud of?

What do you believe about the person staring back at you?

Do you like what you see?

What do you notice about your eyes? Do they look confident, peaceful?

Is there anything preventing you from feeling confident, gorgeous, courageous, or productive?

If your answer to the last question is yes, it may be time to change your limiting beliefs about who you truly are and what you can achieve. Chances are, there are people who look just like you and have successfully achieved their dreams. Maybe you believe you're too short, too dark, too light, too thin, too plus-sized. Or maybe you think that your teeth are too crooked for your dreams.

I grew up with a gap in my teeth. My mom couldn't afford braces. So often we doubt ourselves, and by doubting ourselves, we turn all the reasons why we can't do something into a crutch. There was a time when I thought I wasn't getting a job because I had a gap in my teeth. And for some reason, I thought, *Oh, if I close my gap, get my teeth fixed, it's going to open up a world of opportunities.* In a sense it did, but then I realized that fixing my teeth wasn't a priority. I made history with a gap in my teeth. I was confident enough at that time because I'd done the inner work. I built the confidence because competence had nothing to do with my teeth, despite what anyone—the social media commenters, the kids who teased me in school—said or thought about my teeth. The truth is that *competence is key*. And how the world receives you depends on doing the inner self-work and deciding how you'll present yourself to the world.

There are a ton of examples of people who achieve with this level of confidence. Model Slick Woods does not have a perfect smile and flaunts a huge gap in the middle of her teeth like I did. In 2019, she walked the runway of the *Savage x Fenty Show* with crooked teeth—and while she was nine months pregnant! What if she believed that people with teeth like hers couldn't be models? What if she believed that her teeth were too crooked for her dreams? Instead, she is one of the most recognized models today.

Supermodel Nyakim Gatwech from South Sudan was reportedly and famously told by an Uber driver that she needed to bleach her skin because it was too dark. Thank God she didn't listen! Nyakim Gatwech is now well known for self-identifying as a beautiful "chocolate Black" woman and has become a powerful influencer on colorism. I'd like to go back even further. I'm inspired by Rebecca Lee Crumpler, who in 1864, a year before the Thirteenth Amendment abolished slavery, became the first African American woman to become a doctor of medicine in the United States. What if she had believed that her race, gender, or status in America prevented her from achieving her dreams?

Learn to Spend Intentionally

Ask yourself: *What am I spending on daily that I just don't need?*

Start making intentional decisions about your daily spending. Most of us spend money every single day on stuff that we seriously don't need. Try to identify what that is for you. I'm not saying to get rid of the things that get you through your day and make you feel good vibrationally if it's not going to break the bank; I'm asking you to keep those things and be mindful.

Maybe you spend on venti lattes every day. If that's the case, maybe you can cut back on cost and calories and grab a smaller size? Or grab a latte only every *other* day for a month? *Challenge yourself to get comfortable with the uncomfortable.* You're going to need this kind of control when building financial wellness.

Make a list of things that you don't need to buy daily. Then cut back your spending on these things or make cost-effective changes:

1. _____

2. _____

3. _____

Check In on Your Checking Account!

A simple yet powerful first step you can take toward financial wellness is to take a look at your bank account. You'd be surprised how difficult this is for many people. I find that so many people have a ton of negative emotions surrounding money and finances and are just too scared to look. *You don't need to be fearful about money.* You're trying to attract money! Money is energy, and you can't be afraid of it and attract it at the same time.

Get into the habit of checking your account every single day. Breathe into it if that helps. If you don't like what you see, that's okay—you have the power to make things better. Don't let what you see in your account define who you are as a person. Money is separate from your true value and self-worth. You are a person of value learning to have financial wellness, and your bank account does not define you. You are in charge of it, not the other way around.

An Abundance Mindset vs. a Lack Mindset

Investing in wellness—the health and quality of your mind and body—is one of the most powerful things that you can do to pave the way for wealth. Remember, money is energy. Building financial wellness and attracting money has more to do with your state of mind than you realize.

Do you believe that you deserve to have money?

Do you believe that you can make money?

Do you feel good about money?

What emotions come forward when you think about money?

The truth is—and I can't say this enough—if you don't check in with yourself about the state and quality of your mind, if you don't make space to cultivate mental wellness, if your mind isn't in the right place, *then you're just not going to make good financial decisions.*

Did you ever find yourself making an emotional purchase? Buying something online in the middle of the night to make yourself feel better? Do you have a lack mindset—the feeling that there's not enough?

Some of us, even those of us who have built some financial stability, feel that we may never have enough. We're never satisfied. This is a lack mindset! It leads to an unhealthy relationship with money. You can become jealous of others you see in your neighborhood, or on social media, who present the illusion that they have more than you do, or who do actually have more. You can live above your means to compete with them, IRL or online. But guess what? There are people in the world who have more money than you, and there are those with less. Stop comparing yourself to others and be intentional about investing in your own financial wellness instead.

Cultivate an abundance mindset.

Cultivating an abundance mindset is key. With this mindset, you know that there is enough. You also know there's enough time to achieve long-term goals, to invest and save and plan ahead.

To cultivate an abundance mindset, you may need to change your friend group or block toxic social media feeds. This mindset is something you can't buy, steal, borrow, or counterfeit. You can, however, invest in it.

*An abundance mindset comes from
the inside out, not the outside in.*

Do You Have an Abundance Mindset or a Lack Mindset?

Someone with an abundance mindset:	Someone with a lack mindset:
Is visionary	Is limiting or self-doubting
Is optimistic	Focuses on obstacles
Wants more out of life	Wants more out of life
Sets long-term goals	Lives for the moment
Is not afraid of challenges	Doesn't bother to tackle challenges
Constantly learns new skills	Is unwilling to learn new skills
Is patient with themselves	Beats themselves up
Believes in themselves	Is self-defeating
Is at peace with themselves	Compares themselves to others

Be Intentional with Your Body

In my family we learned early on that what we put into our
bodies has a direct effect on how our body works. Diesel was in

23

the hospital a lot as a kid with many health issues. Pancreatitis was one of them. Every year around Thanksgiving and after Christmas he would get sick if he ate the wrong foods. So besides the amount of food my brother ate, we needed to be conscious of what we cooked and what we served. I think it's important to add that, ironically enough, pancreatitis usually happens to adults who excessively drink alcohol and are forty or older.

Make moments for your body. Support it, whether that's through exercise or just being careful about what you put in it. Are you mindfully eating? I eat when I am hungry. I don't eat just to eat. My typical first meal is usually after 1 p.m. Why? I noticed that if I eat in the morning, I feel nauseous. But there are mornings when I wake up hungry and so I'll eat. There's no precise formula, I'm listening to my body. I want you to check in: Are you eating because food is readily available or are you eating with a purpose?

Take up a new practice that feels good for your body, maybe something like yoga. There are many quick-fix ways to feel good, like going out, taking shots of liquor, eating junk food. By all means live, but don't forget moderation. Seek some balance. Check in with yourself about your body. What will bring you joy? What will lift your vibration? Sometimes, for me, it's eating ice cream, and sometimes it's doing yoga. It's all about balance.

Here are a few practices you can do for your body:

▸ *Go for a hike, a bike ride, or a walk instead of a drive.* Maybe it's just getting immersed in a twenty-minute walk around your city or neighborhood.

▸ *Be intentional about the food you put in your body.* How much food are you putting into your body? Are you actually hungry? Are you just eating for comfort, or to avoid emotions? Are you stress eating?

▸ *Sweat it out!* I've just started embracing the sweat. Go for a jog! Sweating releases toxins, and you'll feel amazing afterward. Wear a hairstyle that allows you to embrace the sweat! You can put on a hat, put your hair back in a slick pony in between salon appointments, wear a wig, or wear your hair in a natural style.

▸ *Make time to work out.* I noticed that the guys on the floor of the New York Stock Exchange would work out at lunchtime. Working out releases endorphins and alleviates stress. You'll be able to conquer the world!

▸ *Work out at home.* If you can't go outside, bring the outside in. You don't need much space or equipment to get in a full-body workout. A ton of free at-home workouts are available online.

▸ *Be in stillness.* There is countless research to back the benefits of meditating. And meditating can come off as intimidating, but really it just boils down to finding moments to yourself to quiet the mind. You can practice moving meditation while working out or going on a mindful walk, or you can meditate while sitting still to focus on your breath. I just want you to find moments where you get in the zone and just breathe intentionally.

−2−

A Five-Year Plan

I'm going to be radical here: have a five-year plan—then crumple it up and throw it away!

When I first graduated from college, I was that girl who was all about a five-year plan. I'd plan meticulously and seriously. Then I learned that life almost never goes according to plan. I've read a ton of biographies of the greats—everyone from Steve Jobs to Kobe Bryant—and a common theme I've noticed is that they never seemed to get *exactly* what they wanted *exactly* when they expected.

You have to go with the flow.

That being said, a five-year plan is absolutely a smart idea. Putting plans on paper is super-powerful as long as you're flexible about them. A plan is a roadmap. A plan is a guide, especially for those moments in life when we're just not in control of events.

Planning to hit the lottery, buy a mansion, meet the love of your life on a dating app, and get married in five years? None of this is in your immediate control. Life happens, but I think that *what is always and absolutely in our control, at any given moment, is our finances.*

I have said over the years, since I was twenty-three, that I would buy a house. I will dedicate a whole chapter to this, but at the start of writing this book and submitting my manuscript I still didn't have my house. Five years later my one goal was yet to be achieved even after having spent time saving and investing. And in real time this felt like an entirety. But it's interesting: once you achieve a goal it never feels like it took as long as it did once it's been accomplished, and it's always gratifying. I believe that we can create whatever we want, with no limits. Five-year plans can be great guides, and having a five-year plan is good for your bigger ideas. But plans may have to change because the reality is that life changes. Be patient with and kind to yourself.

So why make a five-year plan? A five-year plan helps to organize your thoughts. It helps you to better understand who you are, what you want to achieve in five years, and *why* that is important to you. Not why it's important to your family or your friends, but to *you*! If you can understand the reasons for what you want to achieve, then you can be intentional in how you move toward your goals.

There are three important steps to writing a five-year plan:

‣ Write your plan

‣ Protect your plan

‣ Don't adhere to your plan!

Write Your Plan

Your five-year plan should be about what's in your control.

A realistic, flexible guide should reflect your real-life efforts and ambitions. So set some real and obtainable financial goals, such as getting out of debt, or saving a certain amount each month. Or maybe raising your credit score by ten points in a few months, paying off your credit card debt, or putting money toward your student loan debt. Those are goals that are within your control.

Also consider adding other goals such as:

‣ Building your credit

‣ Creating an emergency fund

‣ Opening a savings account

‣ Saving for a vacation in six months

‣ Forming a good budget

▸ Repairing your credit

▸ Building toward living within your means

Your five-year plan should include your wildest dreams. The bigger you dream, the bigger the possibilities. The universe will carve out a path for you. It's not wishful thinking. And if you think it is then you aren't ready to dream limitlessly and you are not in the mindset to receive.

Your five-year plan can include aspirational situations but don't set time limits on your goals.

The time limits for these goals, for example, are not under your control:

▸ Being named CEO

▸ Getting married and having kids

▸ Making a million dollars

I feel like achieving goals within a certain time frame isn't necessarily something you can control. You could be working toward CEO and lose your job tomorrow. But here's the good news: *there are a ton of things you absolutely can control, like practicing healthy financial habits.*

Protect Your Plan

Be confident in your idea.

What if your plans are different from what your parents or your partner or your friends want for you? That's absolutely okay. Be empowered. Not every decision you make has to be okay for everyone else. *It just has to be okay for you, make sense for you, and feel good to you.* If it is, then I say, go with your plan. You can only live your life for you. Don't compare your five-year plan to someone else's. You're not where they're at, and it's okay to not be where they're at. It's okay to be further along, and it's okay not to be. It's okay to be okay with where you're meant to be right at this moment.

Be quiet about your plan.

Don't go around telling everyone about your plans. Keep your plan secret. People will put their opinions, limitations, and beliefs on your plan. You don't want outside influences changing your plans. If you open that door, then you're dealing with people and all of their energy, all of their baggage, and all of their opinions about your plan and you.

Some people are truly supportive, but honestly, you will find that, for whatever reason, a lot of people out there just don't want to see other people win. Perhaps they're projecting their own fears onto you. But when that happens, you can start doubting yourself. You start questioning your plan. *You have to protect your own vision, goals, and energy as much as you can.*

Be a doer, not a talker.

Work silently and diligently toward your goals. In a world where we bare almost all on social media, dare to go quiet. Then, all of a sudden, it's like, oh, you're doing something big, but no one knew. You'll know when it's time to let people know. That will be when you're highly confident that the goal or project or contract has been secured. Until then, no one has to know what you're working on, not even your family.

I've learned that, while I love my grandparents and I love my aunt, they've got lots of unsolicited opinions. So I've learned to not even share with my closest family members. And that is perfectly okay. I've gotten to a very comfortable place where even when I don't have all the answers, I still believe that I'm the only one who knows best what I need to do, what is best for me. So I'm not going to share everything that I'm doing because I just don't want the feedback. If and when I want the feedback, I know to *tap only the people who have been supportive, who can actually help me when I need guidance.*

Sample Five-Year Financial Plan

One Week	Quarterly	Six Months	One Year	Five Years	Manifestations
Make a budget ☐	Save for vacation ☐	Get certified ☐	Repair and build credit ☐	Buy a house ☐	Didn't find home yet, but have the money and credit in good shape for mortgage
Open savings account ☐	Check my bank account ☐	Hire financial planner ☐	Fund IRA ☐	Finish degree ☐	Finished! Hooray!
Save $20 ☐	Pay back my aunt ☐	Save six months of salary in emergency funds ☐	Build my portfolio ☐	Find a mentor ☐	Found a mentor!
Read a book on financial wellness ☐	Pay down credit card bill ☐	Go on vacation with savings; Here I come, Tulum, Mexico! ☐	Save twelve months of salary in emergency fund ☐	Six figures ☐	Not quite yet, but I'm at $80,000
Cut out one unnecessary splurge ☐	Pay a bill that's in collections ☐	Add money to IRA ☐	Get my first apartment ☐	Boat ☐	Shopping for boat, but reconsidering due to boat maintenance costs
Check my bank account ☐	Open an IRA ☐	Save $500 extra per month ☐	Apply for school ☐	Debt-free ☐	I still have debt, but it's good debt, such as a mortgage

Don't Adhere to Your Plan!

You heard me right! Write it down and then let it go. I think what often happens is people get so hyperfocused on adhering to their plan that they aren't open to other opportunities and alternatives. And so they just get near what it is and don't allow life to happen. When you look back in six months, or five years, *you may be surprised at just how much you managed to actually manifest.*

I always liked the saying: Reach for the stars, and you may land on the moon. So let's say your plan is to head your division in five years. You don't quite make it there, but because you're ambitious, you do get a hefty raise. And maybe you realize that your five-year plan doesn't have you working on what you actually love. You might end up changing your plan or changing your job. It's okay that you're not a billionaire in five years. If you believe it's going to happen, it will happen. But how it will probably happen may not be anything that you envisioned at all. It could be even better than you imagined!

Short-Term vs. Long-Term Goals

Short-term goals should be in your immediate control.

Any goal you want to accomplish in less than twelve months should be something you can control because, right now, you've got a job and you know what you make per week, per month, and per year. If you want to save for the next three months for a vacation next year, you know you can absolutely do that. So short-term financial goals are the ones you are absolutely 100 percent in control of, especially after you have your six-month emergency fund set up, have a savings account, and have some debt paid off. Knowing that you're growing and building toward these other goals, you can put extra disposable money toward that vacation.

Long-term goals may take a little longer—be flexible.

Long-term goals require patience, resilience, and flexibility. They're major goals that may be more ambitious and require more work and planning. Maybe you want to buy a house or vacation home, open a shop, or crack six figures. Write these goals down! Magic happens when you put pen to paper.

Give it some time, and check in on your plans.

We should always look back at the plan. Whether I'm intentionally going back to my plans or not, I find that I'm often pleasantly surprised to realize that, oh, I actually manifested a few things! Check in on your plan occasionally to see if there's anything you want to check off as progress and manifestations. But understand that checking in is not so much about being tied to what you initially wrote down as it's about, having set that goal, *celebrating your progress*. Don't beat yourself up if you're not adhering to the plan 100 percent, if what you're doing isn't exactly what you planned. Celebrate that you've been constantly moving toward your goals.

–3–

Networking

Why network? When I think about that question, I always think of my mother, who worked in HR for corporate Home Depot. She would get anywhere between a thousand and two thousand applicants for each job posted on the corporate website. The truth of the matter is that HR professionals within an organization aren't going to interview each one of those people. So you, as a job seeker, can put your application in, but that's not enough. Your chances of landing that job may be one in thousands.

We all know that a job can drastically change a person's life. The stakes are high. You need that job. So how do you stand out? *Networking is the magic formula.* The power of networking and the building of key relationships will make you stand out. Networking is instrumental to achieving your goal, whether that be landing a job, scaling your business, or pitching for funding. Whether you're trying to be an entrepreneur, grow within an organization, or go to a new company, relationship building is absolutely key.

Networking is all about putting yourself out there, period. The internet gives us so much accessibility now. You can literally find probably 99 percent of the people you want to find. And if you can't find them online, know that "six degrees of separation" will help you find someone who can connect you to someone else you're looking for. That said, it does take a little bit of courage, confidence, practice, and endurance to reach out to people successfully.

When I first started networking, I met a guy named Jason, who worked at Goldman Sachs. I reached out to him on LinkedIn. I saw that he had volunteered at the same organization in New York that I'd volunteered at in Georgia. And so I opened the communication when I reached out by saying something along the lines of "Oh, we volunteered at the same place. Can you just have an exploratory lunch with me?" He said, "Yes," and invited me to come to lunch. A few days later, not even in the first five minutes of our meeting, he said, "Goldman Sachs isn't going to hire you."

I had been networking for three months, but it felt like eternity. I'd just started back up again with the negative self-talk, and self-sabotage was starting to seep in. Especially after I was told by a prominent woman who worked in HR, only a few days before, that I was reaching "too high with my goals." Side note: that is single-handedly the worst advice I have ever gotten in my entire life! For everyone reading or listening to this, *there is no such thing as reaching too high!*

I guess it rubbed the lady the wrong way that I was ambitious enough to ask for a six-figure salary in my first job out of college. So at that point, when Jason told me Goldman Sachs wouldn't be hiring me, I was devastated. I don't know if he saw it in my face, but in the same breath he continued: "But there is an equity trading position opening up in the New York Stock Exchange. Would you be open to applying for that position?"

Without hesitation, I said, "Yes!"

I got emotional. I remained composed as we talked, but this was a lot for me because I felt as though I'd been having a lot of meetings filled with promises but no follow-through. People would say, "Oh yeah, I'm going to connect you with this person . . . ," and then there'd be no follow-up. I was starting to think that the problem was me, whatever that might look like. Now, in hindsight, I understand that people are freaking busy. I shouldn't have put so much pressure on myself, but I am an overachiever.

On my way home from that meeting, navigating through New York City to my grandparents' house in Jersey, my phone slipped through the cracks in the subway station. I was devastated, to say the least. The phone contained every contact that I'd spent the last three months building. But in hindsight, I know why. Not why I was devastated, but why I lost my phone.

I was carrying this emotion of *Oh my gosh, yes! I'm excited for this follow-up. But also, is this BS?* So many positive and negative voices were talking in my head, and so my phone slipped through the cracks of the subway. I knew how to get back to my grandparents' house. So that's what I did. I got all the way back to New Jersey, and I just was stone-cold faced the entire time. When I got to my grandparents' house, I was hysterical. I was crying. I was emotional. I was really trying to achieve something bigger than what I had ever envisioned. And I was just putting a lot of pressure on myself. While I was in the middle of having this conversation with my grandparents, my aunt came into the room.

I was thinking, *Oh my goodness, how am I going to get a new phone? I don't have a job. Where am I going to get the money to buy a new phone?* I didn't like asking my family for money. My aunt says to me: "You know, why didn't you get an attendant to go get your phone?" I didn't even know that was a thing.

My aunt went all the way back to New York to the subway station I'd been standing in. She went to the platform ... and there was my phone! With a voicemail inviting me to the New York Stock Exchange the very next day.

I tell this story because, even though I didn't know it, that moment would forever change my life. I am a true believer that when one door closes, another one opens. Things happen exactly when they're meant to, and you can't rush life. You can't rush what you think the end game is going to be. Life is going to play out the way that it is. And you have to be along for the ride and be open to it.

I am forever thankful to Jason, who looked out for me. I am grateful that there was a Black man like Jason who was in a position, and in an industry, to just reach back and connect me. I am so grateful that I didn't give up, because I almost gave up. I was thinking, *I'm probably going to have to go back to Georgia*, on the same exact day that I was offered a job at the New York Stock Exchange; it didn't pay much but I didn't care. This was the NYSE, and the opportunities from there would be limitless.

Networking is your best friend, period. Whether you want to further your personal or business relationships, it is instrumental to adding value to your personal and financial journey. That's why we should all network. Here's how you can get started.

Step 1—Plan Your Network

The first step is to make a list of ten people you would love to reach out to:

1. *Who are your top five high-stakes (H) people?* You're not going to contact the top five immediately because practice makes perfect. Do you have your list of the top five people you're going to reach out to? Great!

2. *Now make a list of five low-stakes (L) people.* Reach out to these low-stakes contacts first, to practice your story. It's important to practice your pitch with low-stakes contacts so that you can reach out to high-stakes contacts with confidence.

Top Five (or Ten) People to Reach Out To

Rank	Name/Title	Pronouns	Company or organization	How do I know or know of?
(Example)	Mr. Donald Brown Vice president	He/him	Lemon Bank	Alumni association
1.				
2.				
3.				
4.				
5.				
6.				
7.				
8.				
9.				
10.				

Low-stakes? (L) or High-stakes? (H)	Social media handles	Phone	Email	Date contacted
H	@DonaldB	646-678-9876	donald@lemonbank.com	
H				
H				
H				
H				
H				
L				
L				
L				
L				
L				

Step 2—Develop a Compelling Story and a Strong Pitch

You have to know what your story is, what your pitch is. Develop your story. It includes your five-star narrative of what you are selling and why you are reaching out. You should have answers to the following questions before you reach out to anyone:

- What is my professional experience and/or lived experience worth? (What does my unique and compelling story bring to the table?)

- What is my financial worth? (How much money do I need to make?)

- What is it that I'm trying to get out of this connection? (Am I looking for a job? A lead? Startup capital?)

- Is this company a good fit for me?

- Why should this person care enough to help me?

Build Your Tribe—Find Your People

I am someone who, coming out of college, didn't have a network. I don't believe in the "woe is me" mentality, but there was definitely a moment when I was like "woe is me." Remember, I'm the first in my family to graduate from college. I wanted to have a tribe around me to really support me, to allow me to vent and to validate my feelings when I needed it. More importantly, I wanted to have people who'd encourage me to move forward. I didn't have these people immediately, so I had to find my tribe through networking.

Find a Mentor

Finding a mentor—someone who is more experienced than you are and who can guide you—is important, but it isn't something that happens overnight. Finding a mentor can be part of a five-year plan, but don't put expectations on it. A mentor usually shows up organically. It's not you reaching out to somebody and saying, "Hey, will you be my mentor?" That's equivalent to asking someone "Will you marry me?" on a first date. It's a bit much. A mentor is someone who will be with you for years to come, and they may not even be in the same line of business as you are. They are your cheerleaders. I don't like to ask for help, so finding a mentor took being open and vulnerable. When I found a mentor, it wasn't intentional. I was fed up and just having an open conversation with someone who ended up being in the position to help me and to connect me to so many other helpful people and resources. I now consider this person a mentor. So don't be afraid to be open and vulnerable, or to ask more experienced people for help or advice with your career.

Diversify Your Network

Your networking group should not be too narrowly focused but should vary as far as age, race, culture, and gender. You may need to leave your comfort zone. As a Black woman, I know that there's just not enough of us in finance positions to form networking groups that look *only* like us, so we have to put ourselves out there. We may need to meet and network with people who look very different from us, and we need to be comfortable with that—comfortable with a diverse group of allies. And for women reading this, as much as it would be nice to have other women's support to lift us up, I have found that that hasn't particularly been my experience. I seek people who will champion around me. Seek to find your allies.

If you're in finance, your networking group should not be made up of just people in finance. If you're in science and you're networking only with people in science, you may be missing out on opportunities because you have no idea who else other kinds of people might know. *So show up as the best version of yourself.* This is someone who is able to network with anyone and everyone, who can let it play out the way it's meant to.

Remember, We Are All "Other"

We've all had the experience of going into a space and feeling like an "other"—meaning we've all come into a room with self-sabotage talk running in our head. You're Black, maybe you're a woman, maybe you're from the South, maybe you are a white man. And for some reason we think that this "otherness" is why we can't connect to the people in the room. I want to call that out and validate that we all come to the table thinking this, and that it's perfectly okay. We identified it. We're calling it out. *Now we're going to use what makes us "other" as our superpower.* We're going to shine being a Black girl, being a Jewish white woman, being a person from the South, and let that differentiate us—and be the reason why somebody wants to bring you on board or network with you.

Know your worth and know the value you add to companies, to people's lives, to friendships. Once you know your worth and your value, actually feel that in your gut and in your intention, then ask yourself: Now how does it feel being the other in the room? It feels irrelevant.

Get Good with Small Talk

Be curious enough to ask questions and know that people love to talk about themselves. If you ask someone a series of rapid-fire questions about themselves, they'll be happy to answer. The more feedback you get, the better you'll understand how you can best connect with them.

An ice-breaking question would be: "So, what made you decide you wanted to go into HR?" You ask questions and allow people to share their story. Find out what's common in their answers and then go from there. The more you work on getting good at asking questions, the better you will be at networking.

Be Strategic

▸ If you can identify what kind of career you want, seek out and join related interest groups.

▸ If you can't identify a clear career path, strategically network with people from many different industries.

▸ Seek out people in hiring positions. I learned this from my mother, who worked in HR: you want to connect with people who can get you into a company. I would say that HR people are your best friends. They are the ones who know the open jobs and can unlock the keys to the company.

Be Flexible

Let's not put judgment on anyone who hasn't clearly identified what it is they want to do by a particular time. According to the Deloitte Global 2022 Gen Z and Millennial Survey, about 40 percent of Gen Zers and 24 percent of millennials wanted to leave their jobs within two years. You can continue to change and grow and learn and understand what exactly the job is that you're looking for. So, while networking, don't get too narrowly focused on a particular job. Be receptive to any opportunities. That's how I got the job on the floor of the Exchange. I wasn't expecting it, but I was open. It's important to grow and learn, but it's also important to stay open.

Networking for Introverts

I think, for introverts, practice makes better. Don't be hard on yourself. If you go to a networking event, don't think that you need to knock out a list of x number of people. If you speak to only one person you really like, but that one person could open doors, then it was a successful event.

Do the Work

Some people think that jobs are just going to come to them. I've heard from a lot of college students who believe that their degree will automatically open doors. That expectation was one of those reality checks for me personally. I realized that I did those four years and still had to work to get a job! I still had to put myself out there. Because the reality was that my college diploma was just a piece of paper. I wasn't getting bombarded with emails from companies saying, "We would love to hire you!" I still needed to put the work in to get a job. The more you put yourself out there, the better.

Be Smart and Safe—Harassment Is Real

If you want to continue growing and developing professionally and financially, you've got to play the game and accept meetings. As a woman, I want to empower other women not to be afraid to go to lunch with someone of the opposite sex. Be smart, though, because *sexual harassment is real*. Let's call it out.

You have to be aware, no matter your gender. You can't always take a meeting in group settings, but you can have a one-on-one meeting in daylight. A lot of deals get closed over drinks. I didn't want to miss out on those meetings, so I would tell the bartender to fill my tequila shots with water. At the end of the day, I was playing the game. I was in the room. Use your best judgment, feel it out. Maybe you can find an ally to go with you to these kinds of meetings.

Set Boundaries

If someone says that they'd like to grab drinks at 8:00 p.m., consider saying: "Oh, I actually have dinner plans, but I can meet you before dinner at 6:30." The closer to business hours you meet up, the less it may feel unprofessional or like a casual date. Absolutely do not go to a closed-door meeting at nine o'clock at night! If someone wants a one-on-one meeting, you can Zoom—and in the middle of the day! Not that things can't happen on Zoom—there are reports of virtual harassment as well—but if you're not in a room with the other person, you can at least feel physically safer. If it feels unsafe, leave. No one has that power over you.

Own Your Power

What do you do if networking makes you feel uncomfortable? At the end of the day, I believe in owning your power. I don't believe anyone has power over you. If it feels like someone is dangling something in front of you, keep a job-seeker face. Whatever they're offering is never worth it. Remember, *you have the power to walk away,* knowing that the right opportunity will come.

I hate that we've made it to the 2020s and women especially still need to be mindful when networking and in the workplace. But always walk away if it doesn't feel good. I'd rather you walk away before putting yourself in a situation where you feel like things have gotten completely out of your control. What is meant for you will be for you. No amount of manipulation or control will stop a person from achieving their goals.

Use the Networking Tools That Best Suit You

Understanding who you are and how you handle various networking tools and strategies is so important. Relationships and connections are everything, so if you are someone who likes to network through building a strong social media presence, that's great. If you're someone who prefers to network in person, then great. *Understand what your superpower is in making connections.*

I'm very intentional with my in-person connections because I know I shine brighter in person rather than just through email or online. That's why I'm so quick to take things in real life and

say, like, "Okay, let's meet in person for a coffee, let's not Zoom."
I feel like I have a magic superpower in person. I've seen people
on the flip side, people who can really do it just completely over
the internet.

A few important tips to remember:

▸ *Be patient.* If you made a connection with someone who
isn't able to help you immediately—for example, they are
unable to introduce you to people, or to get you a job—don't
get discouraged. Put it on your calendar to check in with
everyone in your networking group at least twice a year, so
that you are staying fresh on their minds. Remember, with
networking there may not be immediate outcomes and
everything happens in divine time.

▸ *Don't get discouraged.* When you're reaching out to individuals
and they don't follow up, remember that it's not you—and it's
not them either. Sometimes people are not in a position to
help you out, be your resource, make connections for you, or
give you that job opportunity, even as much as we would like
to think they are.

▸ *Don't take it personally.* Networking is a bit like dating. It kind
of feels like every first date or even like general emailing in
the dating world. Texting back and forth may just fizzle, and
that's okay.

▶ *Say yes to all introductions.* Even if you feel like it doesn't make sense to connect with someone who's not in the same industry, or is building a different career, or earns at a different paygrade, continue to be open to meeting new people.

−4−

Financial Literacy

What do you want for your future? Whether your goal is to build an empire, create generational wealth, or plan for your kid's future, financial literacy sets the stage. *Financial literacy is the foundation to your finances.* You're building your financial house from the ground up. The goal is to have a strong foundation with no cracks that could make it collapse. With a strong financial foundation, you can feel comfortable, safe, and protected during even your darkest hours, knowing that everything will be fine.

Talk About Money

When it comes to financial literacy it's important to be open to having money conversations. If you are part of a family, talking about money should be a team effort in the household. Get your parents to talk to you about money, to start being comfortable talking about money, being vulnerable and open and not making it a taboo subject. The more conversations you have around money, the more solid your financial literacy foundation will be.

There is so much to learn about money. If you don't have anyone in your family to talk with about money, continue to learn on your own. You can listen to a podcast, read a book on finances, and watch videos online. My favorite way to learn is to record the financial channels. When I watch them, I Google everything that doesn't make sense.

Becoming financially literate doesn't happen overnight. Take it slow, and don't be hard on yourself if it's not making sense. Realize that the way you talk about money will change throughout different phases of your life. But I want you to get many different opinions from experts and choose what resonates with you the most.

Identify Your Goals

Having a healthy relationship with your finances starts with identifying your goals, which is really important for the direction of your financial wellness journey. If you don't know what your goals are right now, then you can start by doing a creative exercise that I often share with kids. Whether you're a kid or an adult, this visualization exercise can help you identify your financial dreams and goals.

Visualization exercise

Grab a blank piece of paper or a journal. It's okay if you're not great at drawing; this is only for you. On each side of the paper, draw two large circles. These are your magic mirrors.

In the first circle, draw yourself as a kid. What did you look like? Maybe you had a book bag, or a favorite hat. What were your favorite things? Was it riding your bicycle? Decorating your room? Going to the beach? What were your favorite colors? What did you do for fun?

In the second circle, draw the future you. What does the future you look like? Where do you work? Do you drive a motorcycle, own a pet, or live in a house on the beach?

Okay, so how do you go about becoming future you? *You're going to need money.* You need to understand what managing money looks like. You need to understand the language of money. How do we make transactions? How do we make money? How do we save money? How do we spend money responsibly, and how do we use money for our future?

Start with a Budget

Budgeting and saving isn't easy. It takes twenty-one days to form a habit and sixty to ninety days to form a financial habit. It takes longer because if you are trying to raise your credit score, you aren't going to see these changes happen overnight. Budgeting and saving are psychological: Just think about when you're studying in school for an exam, or working out and trying to gain or lose weight, or preparing for a job interview. It takes practice, consistency, and mental and emotional strength.

I always start by asking people some questions, and some you may have already seen in chapter 1:

▸ What is your relationship with money? Are you using positive or negative adjectives? Using negative words ("I'm needy," "I'm greedy," "I hate money") is a red flag.

▸ What was your parents' relationship with money?

▸ Can you give me examples of people who are good with money? How are they good with money?

▸ Can you give me examples of people who are bad with money? How are they bad with money?

▸ How can you be better with money?

▸ Why are you bad with money?

I ask people these questions because you need to be financially well when you begin to practice and form good budgeting habits. I've talked to people who knew they had a bad relationship with their budget, yet they stayed in that bad relationship even knowing the right tools and steps needed to turn it around. Budgeting takes discipline and sacrifice. You have to stick to the budget as much as possible, even if that means cutting back on your "wants" and spending only on your "needs."

One of the biggest pitfalls is not really understanding the psychology behind why we're not following a budget plan and why we're spending the way we're spending.

One reason why people can't budget and save is typically because they're trying to keep up with the Joneses, the Kardashians, or the Instagrammers.

Create a Budget

Plan your budget after taxes.

When you sit down to plan your budget, understand that it should be based on your income after taxes. That's the biggest mistake people make. I've heard people say, "Oh, I make $50,000 a year." No, you really make $42,000 a year after taxes. You want to be realistic about what you're starting with when you plan your budget. It helps to know the tax laws in your state. Knowing how much your earnings are being taxed and why is very important.

MY BUDGET

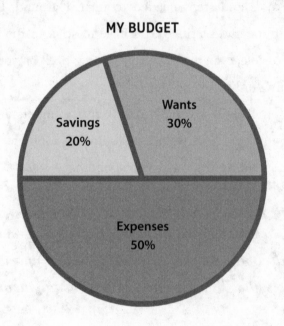

The 50:30:20 rule

A basic budget uses the 50:30:20 rule: 50 percent for expenses, 30 percent for wants, and 20 percent toward savings. Sticking to this formula is a great way to improve your financial wellness.

▸ Fifty percent of your after-tax income is going to go toward your everyday expenses. These are your recurring bills such as rent or mortgage, insurance, utilities, car payments, and so on. If your monthly expenses are totaling more than your 50 percent, it will be really hard to have a healthy budget.

▸ Thirty percent of your after-tax income can go toward your wants. This is your extra disposable money for shopping or going out on weekends.

▸ Twenty percent of your after-tax income is going to go toward your savings, whether that's investing in the stock market, establishing a savings account, or building up an emergency fund that can cover six months of your expenses.

These percentages can be flipped. I actually encourage people to put 30 percent toward their savings and only 20 percent toward their wants.

Keep in mind that this basic budget is not the gold standard. Ideally, people should strive to have an even better budget, one that puts even more toward their future. But by all means, this basic budget is an excellent place to start, especially if this is your first time budgeting and managing your own money.

Personally, I try to save 80 percent of my income, so my budget looks a lot different from one built on the 50:30:20 rule. And I try to keep my everyday expenses below 30 percent of my income. See what works best for you.

Budgeting is personal and will vary based on your goals, income, and expenses and the overall economy. For example, it's more relevant now to follow a strict 50 percent rule because in inflationary times like we're in you may really want to strive to live below your means. Some people are like, "Well, I don't make that much money," and I understand. But I think the sacrifices we make now can really pay off and help build that strong foundation under the sturdy financial house we're building for the future.

Take an honest look at what you can really cut back on. Do you need as many subscriptions as possible? How often are you buying extra things? Get real and honest with yourself. Instead of eating out every single night and going out to the movies, maybe you have a boozy brunch or a movie night at home.

Three years of financial sacrifice now will always pay off later.

The best advice that I ever got from a professor of mine was so good that I made it an affirmation:

The first three years out of college will be
the poorest years of your life.

I stand by that advice today because from there you can only go up! What that looked like for me during my first three years out of college was eating ramen, not going out, and being careful with my spending. But at the same time I was building an empire. I was building my career.

This advice applies no matter what kind of career you're building or whether or not you went to college. It doesn't have to be a traditional nine-to-five. Maybe you're a creative, or an actor, with an untraditional work life. Whatever kind of career you're building, three years to live with less may seem like a long time. But it's a good amount of time to give to making financial sacrifices toward a happy and secure future. This advice works whether you went to college or not. It's never too early or too late to start.

Sacrifice isn't psychologically easy. You have to put your ego aside because social media in the world we live in makes it really easy to compare yourself to others. In those three years when you're making sacrifices, it's really easy to have FOMO (Fear Of Missing Out) when you see, like, "Oh my gosh, they're going to concerts . . . they're traveling the world . . . they're experiencing magical moments."

The world will always be there! You can't really get too caught up in what somebody else is doing. And what I've also learned is that a lot of people pretend like they are doing stuff and they're not. They're coming home to unpaid bills and just not really living a fulfilled life. More than that, some are burning through their money really quickly. In those first three years, while you're sacrificing to build your foundation, they're completely crumbling their foundation and have nothing left to their name.

Check Your Bank Account

The most important thing is doing your research to figure out what works for you and your lifestyle and where you're at today. Take stock of your banking needs and make sure that you open a bank account that works for you. Are you a student? How much money do you make? How much will you deposit monthly? Is it enough to avoid fees?

Look, not every bank works for everybody. Make sure you really do your research. Ask questions. Understand when you'll be charged fees and why. That way, you'll know how to avoid unexpected or crazy banking fees. And remember to check your bank account every single day.

Stay on Top of Your Finances!

We have to be on top of our finances, but so many people are afraid of checking their bank account! You, reading this right now, when was the last time you checked your bank account? How much money do you have in your bank account?

Get comfortable with being uncomfortable. We want to send those fear-based emotions far away. Things done in fear won't lead to results that you want. I challenge you to check your bank account on a daily basis. This challenge will be as transformational for you as it was for me.

We're living in digital times, when it's very easy not to know what is happening with your money because you don't see it. It's very different from how I was raised. I got tangible paper money, and so I could see, *Okay, this was a $5 bill, now I'm down to $1.* I can't stress enough how important this was.

It's really important to know on a daily basis exactly where your money is.

I'll say this again: you have to be bad with money in order to be good with money. When I was younger and less experienced with money, I had moments when I would overdraft my checking account. I never felt good about it. I would always go back and think, *Why did I make this mistake? What did I not budget right?* Answering questions like these is so important. What is your after-tax income? What is your budget? How much is in your bank accounts?

Keep close track of what you spend money on because it's easy to make mistakes. What you spend during the weekend, for example, doesn't hit your account until Monday. So, if you're checking your account on Saturday thinking, *Oh yeah, I did all this shopping within the budget, I have $124 in my account,* you find out when you look at your account on Monday that you actually spent more than you thought. That happened to me a lot when I was younger and would realize, like, *Oh crap, I didn't do that math correctly.*

Here's why financial wellness is so important to me. I've been working ever since I was sixteen. I don't ever really ask my mother for money. And so, in those moments when I made mistakes with my finances, especially when I was younger than eighteen, it was super embarrassing. When I lived in the house with my mother in my early twenties, whenever I would have to say, "You know what? I've messed up. Can you help me?" and, "You know I'll pay you back," it was a super-humbling experience. *Okay*, I'd think, *let me not make that mistake again.* It definitely took me a few times to get it right. This is what I mean when I say that being bad with money will make you good. It doesn't feel good to be bad with money, *and I never want to go back to that feeling.*

Keep track of your savings.

It's important to have a savings account, but you should really look at the savings account as a pulse check. It's a great way to practice managing your money and to establish healthy financial habits. Keeping track of a savings account is good practice. It will let you know how well you're managing your money. Have you checked your account? Do you know what the fees are?

Create an FU fund.

Emergency fund, FU fund, whatever you want to call it, this is your cushion for when shit hits the fan. Flat tire, you're covered.

Dental work, you're covered. This is your "I fuckin' hate my job, I'm quitting, I have enough to walk away, I'll be fine as I look for another job" fund. This is the "Oh my goodness, my parents are absolutely getting on my nerves, I need to move out of this house" fund. *FU funds give you leverage, independence, power, and options.*

Diversify your savings.

Guess what? Your emergency fund and your savings account need to be growing money (aka, growing interest)! So that the $50 you put in your FU fund will turn into $65. Work smarter, not harder, with your money. Put it into short-term money market accounts. Or a series I bond, which, as of the writing of this book, has an interest rate of 9.62 percent, which is higher than inflation.

There is no right or wrong to how you handle your savings, but putting your money in places that don't beat inflation, such as a savings account, is not the best option. You're not stretching your money . . . you're losing the value of your dollar. And you worked far too hard to lose the value of your money. Anything that can grow your money safely, even if minimally, is a better option than just having your money sit.

I am not a big proponent of traditional savings accounts because they don't grow your money in a substantial way. I find that, more and more often, interest rates are not keeping up with inflation. And so that is why, once you have a strong savings account, it's important to diversify your money, to put it into different asset vehicles so that your money can continue to grow. You want your money to work for you.

Whether you're budgeting and saving in a digital world or budgeting and saving with cash, the principles of budgeting and saving are relatively the same. Obviously, if you have your cash just sitting around the house and you're not putting it into financial vehicles, you won't be able to grow your money. Do what makes sense for your life circumstances at the moment. Financial fitness is about developing good habits—remember the 50:30:20 rule—whether you're doing that in all cash or doing that in banks. It's all part of your journey.

Use credit cards wisely.

A lot of people may not think so, but credit cards are your friend. Having good credit gives you access and a cushion that allows you to make higher-end purchases. I'm talking about cars, house rent, utilities, you name it. You need credit and need to learn how to coexist with it. Don't be intimidated by credit cards but use them to set a good foundation for your finances. You need to build your credit so that when you need to use it you can.

An important benefit of having great credit is getting lower interest rates on big purchases, such as cars and houses. Good credit can bring you the lifestyle that you're striving for. But if you have a low credit score, don't let it define you. It doesn't mean that you're a bad person, only that maybe there were circumstances in your life that caused you to slip on your credit score.

I will say that it never made sense to me that interest rates are higher for people with poor credit, especially when so many of them are working three times harder than the next person. But that's the system that has been set up, so we want to be aware of that. We want to make the system work for us. And we do that by understanding the game and then forming the habits to achieve those higher credit scores.

Tips for Building a High Credit Score

▸ *Start early.* If you can, start building your credit before you're eighteen. Ask to be added to your parents' credit card accounts, but make sure that they're financially stable and paying their bills on time so that their good financial habits will help your credit history instead of hurting it.

▸ *Open up a credit card account when you're eighteen.* Don't get too many credit cards because that will actually have a negative impact on your credit score. Start with one or two that have low interest rates or maximum cash back. Find one that works best for you.

▸ *Pay your bills on time.* Pay your credit card bill on time, and pay your utilities and your rent on time as well to boost your credit score.

▸ *Understand the terms of your credit card.* Not understanding the terms and conditions of your credit card can lead to mistakes. Know when the billing cycle ends and know your payment due date. These are two different dates. You won't be charged interest for paying after the billing cycle ends, but you will for missing the payment due date.

▸ *Use incentives to your advantage.* If you have a new credit card that offers incentives such as no interest for twelve months, use this incentive to your advantage. Don't wait, though, until the twelve months have gone by to pay off your card.

▸ *Use credit responsibly and within your budget.* When using a credit card, keep in mind that it is not meant to supplement your income. It is just there to help you when you don't want to pay something off in full. But you do still have to pay for it eventually. That's why budgeting and saving are really important—so that you have the money to pay that credit card bill on time. Also, you may have heard the advice to pay for everything with a credit card. Throughout this book I keep mentioning that it's important to understand who you are when it comes to money. If you know you aren't responsible enough to pay for everything with credit cards, then *don't*. I'm good with my finances, but I know my limits. Paying for everything with a credit card, using all the incentives and perks that can come from using a card—I won't go there, because I know that I could easily fall into bad habits. Do what feels right for you.

Manage and Pay Down Your Debts

Managing your debt is going to depend on what kind of debt we're talking about. Are we talking about credit card debt? Are we talking about student loan debt? Managing your debt is personal, and you have to do what will work best for your situation. Again, it's going to come from that budgeting and saving and maybe even picking up an extra hustle gig to bring in extra income so that you can pay off and manage your debt.

And let me stress this: some debt is a good thing. I don't want you to run away from debt and say, like, "I don't want debt." We all have debt. We have debt when we purchase cars, when we buy homes. Maybe you are in a very fortunate place where you can buy those things outright, but that's not the average scenario.

We shouldn't be afraid of taking on debt, but we do want to be smart about how much debt you take on. So no, you're not going to go out and buy the BMW and then have a $1,000 monthly car note if that's not in your budget. Instead, you're going to make sure that you're taking on responsible debt that you'll be able to pay off. If you take on debt in an irresponsible way, it's going to be stressful. It's going to impact your life. You're going to feel like you're barely floating above water to survive.

There are two ways to pay down your debt:

▸ *Getting debt snowball rolling:* Pay off your smallest debt first, then roll that payment you were making into the next smallest debt. With this method, you gain momentum and rack up those wins a lot faster. You can eventually build toward paying down bigger debt loads. Or you can do the reverse.

▸ *Coming down the mountain:* When you pay off the bigger debts first, you free up money to pay your smaller debts. With the larger debts out of the way, the smaller ones seem easy to just kind of snap your fingers at and pay off quickly.

Live Beneath Your Means

Living beneath your means affords you a cushion of safety in your finances. If your income is $50,000—more like $42,000 after taxes—you want to be living as if you earn $20,000. It's really about making those sacrifices. If you are a person who pays rent, you don't have to sign the most expensive lease. Even with the money that I make today, people have commented that I could be spending four times as much on housing. I find that insane.

I'm like, no, why would I do that? Because my focus is on building for my long-term goals.

A word to my younger readers: don't feel obligated to move out of the family house so early. I know there is so much excitement in moving out on your own. But it is a big financial decision, and once you make that leap it's harder to go back. If your parents are allowing you to live at home rent-free, use that to your advantage. Build your savings and try to put off moving out until you've saved up a year's worth of expenses. I say a year because, if anything were to happen, you'd have a year to recover.

This is advice I followed myself. I know what it is like to be twenty-one and wanting to go out and be an adult, to stop living under your parents' roof. However, I am so grateful I chose not to rush the process, because now I don't have to stress about money. Mental well-being is everything.

Tips on Shopping with Intention

▸ *Buy in bulk at the grocery store.* Inflation is real. Stick to your budget and know what you're actually spending your money on when it comes to food in the house.

▸ *Use DIY cleaning products.* I really like cleaning with DIY solutions. I love to use baking soda to create cost-effective and long-lasting cleaning supplies. For example, you can use a paste of one part hydrogen peroxide mixed with two parts baking soda to clean your bathtub in place of more expensive cleaners.

▶ *Use reusable towels.* Cleaning with reusable towels instead of paper products not only is eco but it saves money.

▶ *Shop for quality, staple wardrobe pieces.* As a young professional at the beginning of your career, you can invest in a basic little black dress or a black or navy suit and wear it every single day. Men can switch out ties. And honestly, even if maybe another woman is like, "Oh, she's wearing the same dress," for the most part people are not really going to call that out. Change your accessories to mix it up. On the trading floor I wore a gray H&M dress that everyone assumed was expensive.

▶ *Invest in a pair of high-quality basic black shoes.* When you choose quantity over quality and buy cheaper items, you often have to replace them because they don't last. It's a better deal to put your money into one quality pair of shoes that will last. You don't have to wear a new pair of shoes on every social media post.

▶ *Shop for bargains.* You can go thrifting or buy quality items at clearance sales. When I worked on the floor of the Exchange, I loved shopping at Nordstrom Rack.

▶ *Presentation is everything.* This chapter isn't about presentation, but it's important enough to take into account in your budgeting and saving. If you need to look good on a budget, remember that tailoring is your best friend. It will make any outfit that looks cheap look expensive. You can get a piece tailored for $20 to $40 and wear it again and again, still looking wonderful because it's been shaped to fit your body.

▶ *Brunch at home with friends.* Going out for brunch can be pricey. Buy your own bottle of alcohol and do boozy brunch at home. Getting together for brunch with friends and family is about the experiences and the memories. Being with your friends and family and making the most out of that is an experience you can have at home.

−5−

Investing

I officially started investing in the stock market right when the stock market crash of 2020 happened. That surprises a lot of people because I had left the New York Stock Exchange two years before. Everyone assumed that while I was on the floor I was investing. But during that time I learned two things: one, 90 percent of the men on the trading floor with me didn't actually invest in the stock market but believed in investing in other areas; and two, I came to really understand what kind of investor I wanted to be. I wanted to feel good about my investments and be confident in my ability to make the best decisions for my own portfolio and not be taken in by all the hype in the media.

There's so much FOMO and hype. You'll hear people say about the latest thing, "You have to be getting into this," and experts in the space saying, "You have to invest in crypto [cryptocurrencies] or NFTs [non-fungible tokens]," or, "You have to be getting into web 3.0 [the third generation of the internet]." At the end of the day, you have to do your own research and make the decisions that work best for your own needs and goals.

What Kind of Investor Are You?

When you have a clear idea of what kind of investor you are, that's a good time to start investing. This is important: *We get so distracted by external voices constantly telling us who we should be, and how we should operate.* Other voices telling us what we should invest in, and why we should invest in them. It's really important to drown out the noise and establish your own clear identity, your own sense of what works for you, and why, and then go from there. To really understand what your goal is, what your intention is, and who you are as an investor. When you're not getting swayed by external voices and not bringing emotions to your investing, then you're in a good place to start investing.

Understanding Your Investing Needs

▸ *Step 1: Understand your risk tolerance.* Are you risk-adverse? Or are you willing to take risks with your money?

▸ *Step 2: What is important to you?* Ask yourself what kind of companies you like. What is your ethos? What makes you happy? What makes you sad? Maybe you don't want stock in a company with a poor environmental track record—you don't want to profit from that. That's probably not a company you want to invest in.

Do Your Research

As a trader at the New York Stock Exchange, I learned that decisions had to be made in microseconds. However many moments we had, we had to own our decision and be accountable, for better or for worse. The same accountability comes with investing.

You will hear the advice that you should invest only in funds, that you shouldn't "stock-pick" (choosing individual stocks instead of an index fund or an ETF). Stock-picking gives you the power to decide which company you want to invest in and potentially leads to larger returns. But I guess the advice out there is to not stock-pick because a lot of people aren't doing their research.

It does take research, really studying the ins and outs of a company, reading their balance sheet, looking at their data. You need to look at how they're doing on a quarterly basis. How much cash is the company sitting on? How much debt does it have? What is its revenue? Is it bringing in more revenue than the debt it's carrying? Doing your research is just looking at the financial health of the company and assessing their future profitability, keeping in mind that past performance does not always correlate with future performance.

Ask yourself: *Is this a growth company or just a company for right here, right now? Is this company a leader today within its space? Will it lead in the future?*

Here's an example. During the COVID-19 pandemic, Peloton exploded, in a good way: the company's stock soared 400 percent in 2020. Peloton was a company that outperformed because, with social distancing, gyms were closed and many people turned to the alternative of buying the Peloton equipment to work out at home. They could even use Peloton technology to participate in virtual classes. High demand during the pandemic brought Peloton strong revenues, but as the pandemic drew on, more companies popped up that were doing the same things Peloton was doing and more. The space became oversaturated, customers had more options, and Peloton's revenue started to drop significantly.

Peloton stock shares plunged 75 percent in 2021. As the pandemic died down, the world started opening back up again and working out at home became less attractive. More people were eager to buy gym memberships and head back to the gym. Peloton is a good example of a company's success being too trendy to be a good long-term investment. It's important to find companies that are strong enough leaders and innovators in their space to hold a strong position in the market over the long run.

No Financial Expert Is Perfect

I want to emphasize that wherever you get your information— whether it's from other people or tips from CNBC or Bloomberg or other experts—at the end of the day we're all human. I say that because we are not fortune tellers. We have no definitive way of knowing what the outcome of the stock market or an individual stock will be, or what an individual company is going to do in the next second, the next hour, or the next day. What we are doing is pulling together all the data out there, all the research out there, and then making essentially a judgment call through our own lens.

I want you to not feel intimidated by experts, to not be afraid to pick your own investments. I don't know all the answers, and neither do the experts. Not to diminish them in any way, but they don't have all the answers because we are all still working with just being human. We cannot predict the future. We're doing the best we can, and sometimes our judgment calls are wrong. Sometimes we completely miss the mark and that's okay.

You're going to make mistakes too when it comes to investing. You just have to own those mistakes and say, *Okay, how do I move forward?* Warren Buffett is famous for reminding us to keep our emotions in check. That's how people get hyped with the crypto mania or with whatever the latest thing is—from investing with emotions. Don't do that: always keep your emotions out of your investing decisions.

Why Invest?

Investing can bring you passive income: income that takes little to no effort or labor on your part to earn, beyond doing your research. Not having to work every day to earn this money will really open you up to new ways of looking at how money can be earned. Gains from investments can also act as a financial crutch for rainy days. That said, I personally don't invest for rainy days but instead with the intention to diversify and grow my money.

How much money do you need for investments?

You can start investing with any amount of money, though a minimum is required for some investments. With services like Robinhood, you can buy $1 worth of stock, which will get you a fraction of a share. For equities, there's no barrier to entry. If you want to invest only $1 and put that into an index fund, you can do that. I would say to start by investing at least $100, but if you can't, then invest with $5. The point is to start somewhere, but obviously the more money you put into an investment, the bigger your return is going to be.

When investing, never use money that you're going to need or miss. I personally don't get it when I hear about people using credit cards or personal loans to invest, or money that they can't afford to lose. That's called leverage trading, which only sophisticated, advanced investors use. Leverage trading is considered highly risky and is rarely used by people in the space. It may give you high returns, but the downside is that you could lose more than you started with. If you have only $5 to your name, why would you invest all $5? That doesn't make any sense. People with only $5 who want to invest all of it on the risk, or the hope, or the chance that they might get $100,000 are doing what we call gambling. And this isn't a gambling book! Seriously, I can't stress enough how important it is to not be investing with emotions. If you are investing with emotions, you have already lost.

Can you invest if you have debt?

When I'm asked by someone whether they should be investing while they're paying off debt, I give them my rule of thumb: only invest within your means. We've talked about budgeting and following the 50:30:20 rule. You should have that 50:30:20 budget established as a foundation for your investing. That 20 percent of your budget is intended to be invested in your future, the 30 percent is your spending money, and the 50 percent goes toward your monthly expenses, which include debt payments.

If you don't have aggressive debt, if you don't have a lot of debt, and if your debt isn't high-interest or revolving (such as credit card debt or substantial student loans), then yes, I would tell you to invest. If you do have aggressive debt, I recommend aggressively prioritizing the paying off of that debt before investing. Again, you have to do what works for your unique situation. There is no one-size-fits-all answer to the question of when is the right time to invest.

Where should I invest my money?

One reason investing your money is so great is that you have so many options. Remember, however, to always do your own research before making investments. In some cases it can even be against the law to take stock advice from those in the know. For example, if someone working at a company has inside knowledge and puts you on to it, this can be considered inside trading.

Here are a few spaces in which to invest.

Education
If earning a degree or certificate from a reputable institution or trade school is going to increase your knowledge and income,

then it can be considered a good investment toward your future. You want to compare a particular school's tuition to the salary potential of the degree or certificate it offers to see if it's the right investment for you.

Stocks

For starters, think of the stock market as a grocery store—a marketplace for buying and selling stocks. When we invest our money in stocks, what we're really doing is buying a part of a publicly traded company. We can buy and sell our shares on the stock market. When its quarterly earnings, which it's legally required to disclose, show that the company is doing well, the value of the stock rises. When it misses its earnings projections, encounters legal troubles, or is the subject of any bad news in general, the company's stock price goes down. You, the shareholder, can choose to buy or sell your stock at any time.

You have to be over the age of eighteen to open a brokerage account. You can open an account in less than five minutes online. Opening an account requires no minimum income or initial investment amount, and there are no fees for accounts that trade equities. Every platform has different offerings; what I look for is free access in order to research companies. Some companies offer dividends, while others do not. Companies that offer dividends are not necessarily superior to others, but dividends are your friend, a source of passive income.

Mutual funds

When you invest in a mutual fund, you're essentially adding your money to a fund collected from multiple investors with common investment needs and interests. That money is invested in a diverse set of investments by a fund manager. Mutual funds can provide tax incentives and are usually considered a lower-risk investment than stocks because of their diversification.

Exchange traded funds

Exchange traded funds (ETFs) are a bit like mutual funds in that they include a diverse set of investments. Yet unlike mutual funds, ETFs are traded just like stocks and can be bought and sold at any time during the day. There are many different ETFs—bond, stock, industry, currency, commodity, etc. When you buy stock ETFs, you're buying a basket of companies. There is a big difference between owning a stock and owning a stock ETF: with a stock you own a share of that company, and with a stock ETF you own a fraction of that company along with other companies.

ETFs are a good option if you don't want to sit down and do the research on individual companies. And they are generally good for people just starting out. You can invest as little as $5. The rule of thumb when it comes to investing—not to encourage spending more to invest more—is that the more money you put into investing, the greater your potential return. Also, ETFs are tax-efficient, which means that you will lose less of your gains to taxes.

401(k)

If your job offers a 401(k) plan, it's important to know how that works. Essentially, a 401(k) is an employer-sponsored account. You make contributions to the account directly from your paycheck, and up to a certain amount your employer matches your contribution. You have a smaller paycheck and less cash in the short term, but the money invested is definitely being saved and potentially gaining value with every withdrawal from your paycheck as you build up your account to meet your long-term goals.

A Traditional IRA and a Roth IRA

An IRA is an individual retirement account. There are two types: a traditional IRA and a Roth IRA.

Contributions to a traditional IRA are made pretaxes, while a Roth IRA is used for after-tax contributions. You do pay taxes when you add money to a Roth IRA account, but then you can take out the money tax-free after a certain amount of time, usually five years. So a Roth IRA may be better for long-term goals. The money in either account can be put toward other investments such as stocks, bonds, ETFs, and mutual funds.

Commodities

A commodity is a tangible material. Corn, oil, agricultural products, lumber, and gold are all commodities. You can invest in commodities by purchasing the actual material, such as gold, but such acquisitions are costly and hard to store. You can also buy commodities through options, aka contracts. I personally don't invest in commodities, since commodity trading is usually focused on the short term and I play the long game. Commodity trading may be right, however, for some people. Commodity trading can sometimes be used as a hedge during volatile market conditions, depending on circumstances.

Alternative assets

Here's a secret from high-network individuals for investing and growing your money: they invest in alternative assets. My mother, who is very intentional with her money and doesn't go crazy on splurges, bought me my first Chanel bag when I graduated from college. That bag, bought for about $6,000 in 2016, is now (in 2023) worth about $11,000. If I needed to sell my bag, I could make a $5,000 return on my mother's investment.

Investing in things such as Rolex watches, fine wines, fine art, handbags, and shoes can be an option. I have seen Pokémon cards, Beanie Babies, and sneakers gain in value. Remember that doing your own research will show you what has potential to grow in value and what doesn't.

Crypto

"Crypto" is the hot topic at the moment. For people who may have not heard of crypto or still don't really understand what crypto is, it is a digital currency that works on the application of blockchain technology. Blockchain technology records transactions across many computers and the blocks can't be altered or changed. I am an advocate for blockchain technology. People often confuse crypto with blockchain technology and think that they are synonymous but these are completely two different things. To put it in simple terms, cryptocurrency is a digital currency and blockchain technology is the computer behind it.

With crypto, you don't have to rely on banks to verify transactions. It is a system where you can send and receive payments. It is not a tangible item, as you cannot physically touch a crypto. I fully believe that a global digital currency is necessary as we are moving into a digital world. We are already in this world where we are seeing a physical cashless society, a physical cardless society where we are tapping to pay and even using the palms of our hands to pay, and so evolving into a digital currency only makes sense. The first cryptocurrency was Bitcoin, founded in 2009, and it has the largest brand awareness. I believe Bitcoin will stay around. Because crypto works on blockchain technology, I do believe that we will see a future where all financial transactions will be traded using blockchain technology, including stocks, bonds, and other financial assets.

Crypto doesn't have any intrinsic value; it is backed by supply and demand. Everyday people contribute to its worthiness, which is why we see large ups and downs when it comes to the value of crypto. For people who make the argument that money such as the US dollar is backed by gold, that is a dated misconception. Today, globally, no national currency is backed by gold. They are all on a fiat system, meaning it is backed by its country's government, not a physical asset. To put that into perspective, your country's central bank has control over its money and its economy.

Crypto wants to be the opposite and not be centralized. Because as with anything, you will have bad players who mess it up for everyone, I truly don't believe as a society, in the US or even globally, we can operate without centralized banks. With recent developments of the crash of crypto and the many bad players involved, the argument for crypto to be centralized has only grown. This is all the good I can say about crypto and the case for why we should be paying attention.

Here is what I will say: If you understand what kind of investor you are, and if you have done your research and are not just following someone on social media but really sat down to read opposing arguments and understand the risk, then shoot for the moon. The most important thing is diversification with investing, whether bonds, cash, commodities, equities, alternative assets, or potentially crypto.

It is too early to call the future of crypto. Today, in 2023, crypto is not a hedge against inflation, and its market crashes have been far more substantial than the S&P 500's.

I recently read an article on crypto saying that the crypto crash disproportionately impacted African Americans compared to their white counterparts. Why? Because, when it comes to investing, you cannot lead with emotions. Crypto is not the first alternative asset to come along that has gotten people really excited and really eager to put their money in it, with the idea that they would get rich overnight. The goal is not to get rich overnight, which would be nice but is just not realistic. *The goal is to create generational wealth and achieve financial wellness. This does not happen overnight.*

So often with these new alternative assets that become accessible to anyone and everyone—including the recent hype around crypto—the people profiting from it have already made their money by the time you're hearing about it. African Americans are twice as likely to still invest in crypto and not believe that there are any risks involved. At the same time, they just aren't diversifying their money enough. They're putting a large percentage in crypto instead of stocks, bonds, mutual funds, etc. I'll just say this: if it sounds too good to be true, it probably is. And diversifying your portfolio is a goal that we should be always striving for.

Perhaps in a few years or a decade, crypto will be completely different. Then you can all come back and write me and tell me that I was wrong. But for now, I see it negatively impacting my community. Crypto is causing people who already don't have money to have even less money. *Do your research! Get opposing ideas!* There is always some truth in the opposite argument. There are a lot of bad players who have been involved with crypto and are scamming people. I want to just say again that there is a need for a digital currency. But for me to invest, I'm still watching on the sidelines on how things continue to develop.

Life insurance

A life insurance policy is a contractual agreement between a policy-holder (the insured) and an insurance agency. The policyholder pays a monthly or annual premium to the insurance company. If the policyholder dies, a sum of insurance money is paid out to the designated beneficiary chosen by the policyholder, usually a family member.

I've been seeing a lot of life insurance policies on social media being used as an investment tool. Life insurance policies are meant to protect families, preserve capital, and provide stability when someone passes away. Who are life insurance policies best for? People who have dependents. I am saying that you will never hear of a wealthy person who grew their money by buying a life insurance policy. So no, don't invest in a life insurance policy with the expectation that it will grow your money.

Find a Financial or Money Coach Who Works for You

If you're not comfortable investing on your own, you can hire someone to help. A financial adviser can be a good asset to use, but don't just pick the first person who comes to mind. You should interview several candidates before deciding. You have to like your adviser and be confident they're working for you. I may not vibe well with an adviser who can't understand where I'm coming from and who is not looking at my goals through my lens. I'm the first woman in my family to go to school. My needs are going to be a lot different because I essentially come from no net worth, no wealth. And so some potential advisers just may not be the right fit. It's worth finding the right fit so that you and your adviser are on the same page.

Money coaches are also helpful and not as costly. They mostly will guide you to help you budget and save or tackle debt. Money coaches aren't licensed, but that doesn't necessarily mean that they can't be helpful. Still, I would remain mindful of any red flags. Here are a few frequent red flags to consider.

Red Flags

▸ *An adviser or coach who makes guarantees:* Here's the thing: anyone licensed in the financial space will never guarantee anything. We use words such as "potentially," "possibly," "likely," etc." Never extreme absolutes. As someone who was once formally licensed—currently I don't directly work for an organization regulated under the Financial Industry Regulatory Authority (FINRA), an organization authorized by Congress to protect investors—I am still mindful of the language I use. Use of language such as "100 percent guarantee" by a potential coach or adviser is a red flag.

▸ *An adviser or coach who offers to build your credit:* I am in the process of buying a home and I have this blemish on my credit from five years ago due to one missed late payment. The conversation with the recommended money coach started this way: "Lauren, you have great credit! There's really nothing here to work on [*pregnant pause*] . . . but you do have this blemish. I can 100 percent fix this for you, and this could absolutely raise your credit by forty-five points." "Okay," I said, hesitantly. "Yeah," he continued, "I can have this removed for a onetime up-front payment of $599." I was referred to this man, oddly enough, by my potential lender. You should have been there to witness my face. Something didn't sit well with me, and it wasn't just the outrageous price. Immediately following the call, I did a quick Google search. Someone who says they can wipe an *accurate* credit blemish off your credit report is lying. Also, it is illegal. Per the Consumer Financial Protection Bureau, it is illegal to ask for money up front; anyone offering to help you build credit should ask for money only once the service has been completed. In my case, "completed" would have meant the blemish was removed and my credit score had gone up forty-five points.

▸ *An adviser or coach telling you that you can't reach out to credit report agencies directly:* To take care of any credit discrepancies, you *can* reach out to each credit bureau directly, and *for free*.

– 6 –

Investing in Real Estate

Real estate is an alternative asset, but I thought it deserved its own chapter. Owning a home has long been a huge part of the American dream. I always wanted to own a home, but it had to make financial sense. You will hear some people say that real estate is the be-all and end-all investment, that you can make money on real estate if you invest wisely. You can buy an investment property, fix it up, and flip it, like we see on HGTV. Or you can invest in a rental unit that's going to bring you added passive income. You're also responsible for putting money toward maintaining that property, though, so you have to do that math.

If you live in the home that you buy, the long-term appreciation in your property value is going to depend on so many different things, like the real estate market, the neighborhood you purchased in, the terms of your mortgage, and interest rates. That's why you really need to do your research and look at your needs.

Sometimes it may make more financial sense to rent than to own and to build your wealth in other investments—for example, if mortgage rates are high, or if the property is selling for more than it's actually worth at the time you go to buy. Also, if you can't outright buy real estate, you can always invest in a real estate investment trust (REIT). This provides you with dividends (aka passive income), and its performance isn't subject to larger stock market conditions. Also, you don't have to worry about the upkeep of a home. Someone else is managing it for you.

I was fortunate, as my mother was able to own the home where we grew up. That was an important investment to her. Keep in mind that homeownership for Black Americans hasn't been easy due to a number of reasons including institutionalized racism. Black people in America own homes at a rate of 46.8 percent, compared to 75.8 percent for white Americans. And homes in Black neighborhoods are valued at $48,000 less than homes in mostly white neighborhoods. It's not fair and amounts to a loss of about $156 billion of equity for Black homeowners. This makes up a huge part of the racial wealth gap. But we're not here to let any obstacles real or perceived deter us from achieving our dreams and goals.

The Great Debate: Buying vs. Renting

I've noticed a great debate online about whether it makes more financial sense to buy versus to rent a home. As I've said before, investing is personal and so anyone who feels they may save more money by renting should totally do so without shame. There is evidence out there to support any argument or theory in this debate. I've seen experts online say that buying is the minimum you will pay a month for housing, and renting is the maximum you will pay a month. I've heard others say that paying rent will have you spending less out of your monthly budget than buying, or that it costs more to own a home monthly than it does to rent one. I agree with this in theory, because, yes, today it may cost less to rent; however, as it seems rent prices are steadily rising every single year, if you bought a house today your mortgage payment won't increase in ten years, while the rent for the apartment will increase next year, and every year after that.

You'll hear some naysayers mention that you aren't just paying a mortgage when you own, you are also paying insurance, taxes, and unexpected household expenses. All of that is true but it's true with most big purchases. If you purchase a car, you'll have to pay additional insurance, and you might have to replace a tire or the engine. In life unexpected expenses happen. It's a part of life and so it's important to have an emergency fund to cover those unexpected housing expenses. Please don't allow that to be a deterrent to buying a home.

My Home-Buying Journey

At the start of 2022, I had just moved into this beautiful high-rise apartment building with floor-to-ceiling views of the ocean. Every apartment that I lived in prior to that apartment was an upgrade from the last. And I loved my apartment, but I was ready to own. So, I set an intention at the beginning of 2022 and said, "I am buying a house this year!" Now in fairness, I'd been saying that for the last five years. However, there is a big difference between saying an intention and *feeling* your intention.

I realize that the true reason that I didn't have my house after five years was because of me. Contrary to my own best advice, I had set a goal and I wasn't willing to be flexible. My goal was to buy my house fully with cash. Why? I saw it on the internet! Seeing all of these people offer to buy homes fully with cash, to avoid having a monthly mortgage expense, made me want to do the same. While I hadn't achieved the dollar amount that I needed to buy my home with cash, I did have quite a savings for a down payment because I'd saved so aggressively. Once I became flexible on that goal, I was able to manifest my house.

Steps to Buying a Home

Have a vision.

My process started with just touring homes, and it didn't matter the price point. Not that I didn't need a budget, because even billionaires need budgets. I toured all price points in person to raise my vibrational energy. I also wanted to get a better idea of the housing market and what homes were out there. I wanted to understand what was important to me when it came to buying a home. Square footage, rooms, yard, pool, location, etc. I knew my home would be an upgrade from my apartment. When I lived in Brooklyn, I had the entire view of the borough from the twenty-ninth floor. A view was priority one, along with being spacious so my brother could ride around the house in his wheelchair with ease and have access to most things in the house. I was less picky about the style of the house and whether it was modern, classic, Spanish, etc. I just knew I wanted that view, floor-to-ceiling windows, and a comfortable place for my brother.

Find a good realtor.

I am through and through a businesswoman, and I knew for a fact that I would not purchase any home over ask price or at ask. When I started my journey on purchasing a home, interest rates were low, and people were notorious for buying homes over ask. I just couldn't fathom doing so with a realtor who should've understood that was tricky. Finding a realtor who understood my goals and who wasn't trying to project their goals on to me was a dance. If they weren't in alignment with me, then they weren't for me, it's that simple. Most realtors were advising me to be aggressive with my offer. And yet in the back of my mind I knew that what is meant for me will be for me. I was often told by realtors that within my price point I wouldn't be able to find a home within my budget, that I would need to find a condo instead, but I didn't believe them. I said *nope, it's out there.* It was so important for me to find a house for my brother.

Have faith in the process.

In the process of buying my home I followed Gabby Bernstein's advice on asking the universe for a sign when it came to knowing if a certain house was for me. It's simple if you are unsure of a decision you want to make and want to be reassured you are on the right path. The sign can be anything; for example, you can say:

"I want to see a blue bird."

"I want the number 11 to appear."

"I want to get a phone call from my distant cousin."

100

Whatever that sign is, that is your answer; if you don't get the sign, then that as well is your answer. The funny thing is my sign was a rabbit. And I saw rabbits at three different homes that I toured. I toured over a hundred homes but there were three absolute contenders. I took that as well to mean that maybe I can't go wrong with any of these homes, but there was one home that I just knew was mine. I called it the "black kitchen house." It was modern and had this grand front door with a beautiful view. And I went back to this house several times.

Put in an offer.

I finally put an offer on the house. It was lower than the ask, and I was filled with nervous emotions because I didn't want to offend the owner. Remember that what we put out into the universe we receive back. I put the offer in, and a month went by and all I received was radio silence, which isn't normal, as you'll typically get a response within a few days.

Finally, the realtor got back to me and said the owner was so appalled by my offer that he went into a depression. Ouch. That was when my fear turned into reality. But she advised me to let him sit on my offer and in the meantime to keep looking for homes. "I really believe he will come around," she'd said. So, I did just that even though I felt reluctant. This black kitchen house

I just loved! The only other thing I wanted to add to this house was a lemon tree in the backyard. But the house was not priced correctly, which is why I felt I was in a good position to offer the price that I did. When it comes to a listed home, if it is priced correctly or even below you will in many cases in any economic environment see multiple offers on the home. If a house is sitting, then something isn't as it seems.

After weeks, and no other offers on his house, the owner came back and gave me a best and final counter on my price. It was significantly higher than my initial offer. After crunching the numbers, I had to let the house go. This house, even with the signs, wasn't my home. The surrounding comps in the area didn't justify the price along with the rising interest rates and what my monthly payment would be. And something about this house sitting for three months in an environment where homes wouldn't even last a day or two on the market also concerned me.

At this point interest rates had gone up even more causing my intended price point on homes of interest to dwindle. At this point in the process, I had a real conversation with my mom, saying, "I'm only going to look at one more home and when my lease ends if I don't have my house, I will move back to Georgia for the time being." I was energetically in a low place and heartbroken over my black kitchen house. But I had to believe that what is meant for me will be for me.

Keep searching.

The following day there was a house that was listed online that had zero photos posted but a 3D model of the home that showed the view from the back of the house. The view had endless mountains. I looked over at my mom and said, "Mom, I think this house is my house." I was so matter-of-fact about it that it was scary. The next day I showed up at the house, and it was vibrant with color as there were so many flowers around the house. I walked up the grand staircase, through the grand iron-rod front door, and I knew immediately again *this is my home*. Without even looking at all of the bedrooms and just cutting my eyes directly across the living room to the views of the mountains I knew this was my home. I knew I could spend my days in the backyard meditating, journaling, doing yoga. There were hummingbirds dancing around the house. This house was magical. Maybe it would seem small to most of you reading this book, but it is big to me.

In this process of searching for homes I told my mom a few days prior, "Wow, on this journey I have yet to meet one Black female realtor." It wasn't the be-all and end-all, but just something I was aware of. As I was touring the home, I made my way to the final room where the listing agent stood, and she was a Black female realtor. It felt so right to see her. The universe was reassuring me.

The next day I put an offer in on the house, as I did not want to sit and wait. The house, in my opinion, was priced a little too low. So low that my agent thought there must be something wrong with the house. The elderly woman who was selling the house had just bought the house less than a year prior; it was just her. After living in the house she felt that it was too much house, so she bought another house and was eager to get rid of this house immediately. She didn't care about making a profit, she just wanted to unload it. Talk about fully being in alignment! I put my offer in below ask for a house that was already priced too low and within twenty-four hours she accepted my offer.

Believe in housing magic.

I asked for a sign to show me my house, and you know what's interesting? Yes, I saw a rabbit. And while I was in the black kitchen house, I also saw a rabbit but it ran *behind* the house. I didn't realize that the rabbit I saw that day was running toward my new home, which sits directly behind the black kitchen house.

I continuously see signs related to my dream home on a daily basis. My favorite book growing up as a child was the *Secret Garden*. I always wished I had a home that was filled with all the beautiful plants described in that book. And guess what? My new house is engulfed in pink, red, orange, white, and yellow roses. I also have fuchsia camellias everywhere. Birds of paradise line my backyard along with an entire wall covered in green vine. There are also palm trees. I never asked for a pool, but it also has this nine-foot-deep, blue, 40,000-gallon pool, which is a bonus that this house has that the black kitchen house didn't. But the kicker is that one day I was walking around the landscape and noticed that I have a lemon tree in my backyard. This home is everything that I asked for and more.

Buying the house was also a good investment. I offered below the ask, and got additional credits on the house after installing new floors and fresh paint. My house is now easily worth half a million more than what I paid for it. So, if I were to sell my home today, less than six months after purchase, I would make half a million dollars on my investment. How? Well because there were many homes surrounding my house that sold for more than the price of my home and are smaller in square footage. Some of the properties don't even have a pool or a view. With all that combined and more, my house has appraised for over half a million dollars more than what I paid for it.

Yes, I am aware that these numbers might sound inconceivable but it's not impossible to achieve. There is a reason why generational wealth is built with real estate, because the money you make by owning property can set you up for years to come.

I want you to go online and search a home, an older home, one that has history, and just go back and look at the progression of what someone listed the home for in the year 2000, what it sold for, and its current list price. I'm currently looking at a home in Newark, New Jersey; in 2009, it was listed at $89,000 and sold for $100,000—that's $10,000 over ask. That same home has now been relisted in 2023 for $419,000. That means if this home sells at list price the owner of this home has made $22,785, 29 percent annually each year for the last fourteen years. You will not see returns like this by investing in the stock market only, which gives 8 percent return over ten years. Yes, if you buy today you won't find numbers as low as they were in 2009, but you are thinking about the future, the investment.

Beyond the money, it was me holding back tears as my brother came to visit the house for the first time and him just being so in love with the house and his room. That was priceless. Memories are priceless.

Now the reality is, I have an older home. In my first month there were things that I had to pay for that I didn't account for, and the down payment on this home ate my savings. But after the shock and unexpected expenses I know this was hands down one of the greatest investments I have made and it's all mine. If I want to move to another state, I could put this on the market to sell, or rent it out and get passive income. Yes, it took a while to get here. Longer than my five-year plan, but the way it happened, my end result, I would do this process repeatedly.

Look for help.

I want you to know that there are programs here in America for first-time homebuyers to have access to purchasing homes that require no credit score and no down payment. Again, I have said this throughout the book: don't let your "other" be the reason why you think you can't do something. Everyone loves to throw the statistics out there, loves to remind you that buying a home as a minority is hard. And it's important for that information to be out there so that inequities can be addressed, but it's not your affirmation. Your affirmation is:

I intend to buy the home of my dreams.

Don't put a time frame on it, just allow it.

Don't worry about how you will get the money. The money will come. Focus on the house. All you need is to believe, throw it out to the universe, continue to make your money move, and everything else will fall into place.

One more story to share is about my grandfather. Right before I bought my house, I was an emotional wreck. I was crying because it's hard for me to part with money, and I was about to part with more than I ever have had to part with before. And I was also about to make a twenty-year commitment. He shared this beautiful story about his first home, the home my grand-parents bought together. He'd toured a house that he knew he just couldn't afford but thought it was perfect for his wife and kids. He wrote the check for his down payment but asked during escrow if they could wait to cash the check. A few days later he got a call to come pick up the keys to his new home. He thought that was weird, as he knew he didn't have enough money in his account for that check to go through, but sure enough he went to the office to pick up his keys. After the close of his house, he had less than $20 in his bank account but he knew that around the first of the month the money always showed up in his account. All that to say, my grandfather looked at me and said,

"This is new for you, and this first home purchase will seem scary and the first with anything is always a bit scary because of the unknown. You will be okay. You are supported."

I needed to hear that from Grandpa, and I want to share that with whomever needs to hear that. You are supported. For all my readers, I am manifesting for you. "You have the house of your dreams, and you are financially supported." A win for you is a win for all of us.

–7–

Diversity, Equity, and Inclusion

Working in an industry where Black women like myself make up only a small percentage of the workforce, diversity, equity, and inclusion (DEI) have been up front in my career. Men dominate the C-suite, with women, especially Black women, falling behind 80 percent in upward job mobility within the financial industry.

As the only woman on the floor of the New York Stock Exchange, I was occasionally faced with gender and race issues, issues of sexism, and a lack of diversity within my circles. I have always been vocal whenever I felt empowered to be that way, but in some situations speaking up has been a waste of time. Institutions and organizations in power have to have the *intention* to see change.

That's why I believe the conversation around diversity, equity, and inclusion as it pertains to mind, body, and money is a powerful one. Remember, poverty and a general lack of economic power in communities of color lead to so many social, environmental, political, and even health disparities. We have the power to change the conversation around DEI through financial wellness and literacy.

Spend Intentionally

Purchasing power is everything. We have the power with our money to make certain changes within organizations: how they're structured, how they treat women, how they treat Blacks, how they treat the LGBTQ community. We just really have to be all about that. I don't care if it's convenient to go and spend your money with corporations such as the giant low-cost retail stores that show up in every poor and middle-class neighborhood in America, because maybe they don't go out of their way to support the communities they're doing business in. Maybe they're giving the money you spend in their stores to politicians who vote against your political and personal interests and human rights. Why do I need to help them get richer when I get no type of gain from it? I don't think that our buying power should be one-sided. Using our buying power is a transaction, and in a transaction *both sides benefit from the exchange.*

In 2022, CNBC's Frank Holland reported that Black spending

power had reached a record $1.6 trillion. That should be good news, right? The Black community's ability to buy intentionally, save money, and invest nearly doubled between 2000 and 2022. But meanwhile, the net worth of Black communities declined by 14 percent. That means that Black Americans had more debt than assets such as real estate, stocks, and bonds. BET founder Bob Johnson, a respected Black entrepreneur and businessman, suggested that Black people need to rethink how they spend their money.

We can't disregard the long-standing systemic issues facing the Black community, such as housing injustice, predatory lending practices, banks' refusal to make loans to Black businesses to expand, systemic racism that reinforces glass ceilings at work, and the straight-up destruction of thriving Black financial communities such as in the Tulsa race riots of 1921. The history is heavy. Looking forward, we have to understand that, today, $1.6 trillion is a huge opportunity for Black communities to begin to spend intentionally right now. We *can* invest and save, we *can* buy stocks and bonds and homes and ETFs rather than throwing our money away on purchases that don't increase in value. This is how we can build a more diverse, equitable, and inclusive conversation in our communities. Financial literacy and wellness can lead us to empowerment today. We have to spend intentionally, we have to make smart investments, and we have to think long-term.

Invest Intentionally

It's good to spend and invest in companies that align with our personal goals and ethics as well as those of our community. Money is power. The way we save, invest, and build our wealth and start building generational wealth makes us a part of the conversation. As part of the conversation, we can hold politicians, corporations, and government entities accountable for the diversity of their hiring practices, for the economic and environmental impacts of their products and actions, for their approach to LGBTQ rights, antiracism, and women's rights, and even for their stance on maternity leave.

Some people will just not eat at certain chicken franchises because of their lack of diversity practices. You have to put your foot down; you have to call out companies like that and say, "I'm not going to support this business." I think what history has shown us is that changes are made when we really are intentional, when we withhold our money and use our voices.

I think for some people it's just convenient to be able to order from the local restaurant of a corporate pizza chain. It does take a little bit more energy to locate and support a woman-owned company or to find and go to a Black-owned nail salon. It takes a little bit more research, but I think the value of it is important. Building up those businesses instead of contributing to the bottom line of organizations that don't align with our values is important;

we need to continue to weave that ecosystem around us. I think that we're slowly getting it. We're beginning to understand our power, using social media to speak out. Again, you have the power as an individual to question hiring practices. Don't be afraid to speak up. Don't be afraid to call out organizations that ignore your DEI concerns.

Work Intentionally

A few years ago, while I was preparing to move away from the New York Stock Exchange, I had interviewed with many top-tier financial firms. There was one in particular that kept asking me to come in for additional interviews. I liked the company. I liked the people. I appreciated how they had four-day workweeks, prioritized time off, and required employees to take at least twenty-one days off a year. Everyone seemed to really like the company and the job that they were in. And they weren't overselling the company; their feelings were genuine. But for some reason I just couldn't commit to working for this company. Something seemed off.

So finally I asked the hard question: "How many people of color work in your organization, or, more specifically, in the C-suite and above?" And they said, "Four." Pause. This is a global company. We aren't talking about a company with fewer than one hundred employees; we are talking about a company with well over one hundred *thousand* employees in over fifty countries. "We are working hard on our diversity and inclusion efforts and have even created an entire DEI department to make sure we make that happen." I told them, "Listen, come back to me in a year, and we can have a conversation. Let me see the numbers then, and maybe I'll feel good about being an employee of your company."

In the year 2023, there just isn't any excuse for companies to not be more diverse. They should have a diverse representation of employees, period. When I see organizations that have less than 1 percent employees of color but are "working to improve this," that is a red flag through and through. There are Black people, Latinas, Asians, and women everywhere, and saying that you're trying to "find us" is insulting in itself. We aren't hard to find; you pass us on a daily basis, especially in big metropolitan cities. There just isn't any excuse for lack of diversity in a workplace. But this story gets better.

After a year, as promised, I reached out again to the recruiter and head of HR at this company. I was asked to come in, but the recruiter insisted that we meet for lunch beforehand. I was told that they had "dissolved" the position I applied for earlier, because they didn't deem it "necessary." I laughed out loud. I'm giving you the details of my experience with this company to say not only that we should definitely hold companies accountable for their lack of diversity, but also that you don't have to work for a company that doesn't want you. Period.

Gen Z, I commend you. You have more entrepreneurs than any other generation, and you're making more money than the generation before you, the millennials. You understand the importance of a diverse workforce and making that an intention. Long gone are the days when we had to work for companies that just didn't care about us.

But before you write off any company that is lacking, I will share this. One reason I liked Rosenblatt Securities was that Mr. Rosenblatt was making a larger effort to diversify the company's hiring practices. It came up in our conversations. Prior to this effort, they had been hiring within their network. Everyone who worked there had been referred by someone in the network. This was the way it had been done for years—through word-of-mouth referrals from school classmates, cousins, former colleagues, and others in their network.

So it's about who you know as much as anything else. That's why building your network is so important. The problem is that, when your network is not diverse, a company may fail to pull in really diverse talent this way. That's why it's so important that companies reach out to communities of color, to women, to LGBTQ communities. Sometimes they're going to find these talented and diverse individuals outside of their usual network.

But I don't want people to walk away from this book thinking, "Oh, white men are not allies." There are white men who can be allies. Some white men are absolutely allies, and they don't want anything in return. I want to call that out. I know sometimes I get really riled up about DEI, and I'm all about it. But I want people to understand that some white men have really looked out for me, and there are white men who will look out for you. I've gotten to every point in my career because of a man, and many of those men were white. There's no need to look at all white men as an enemy. Those who are meant for you will be there for you, and they will be champions of your success.

It's important to keep an open mind and seek the best in people, even white men. If they disappoint you, then you know who your allies are. I'm intentional with talking about white men here because, unfortunately, as of 2023, they still hold the majority of power and influence.

The intention to recruit diverse talent has to be sincere. I've found that some companies have no real intention to diversify their hiring and instead are just going around in circles. It's a waste of time for you to even attempt to get this kind of company to change. But again, this is why we have to ask ourselves: *Do we want to support organizations that don't align with our interests and don't give back to our communities?*

– 8 –

Asset Classes

If you're going to grow your money, you need to understand what kind of economic environment we are currently in. So, if you come back to read this book in two years, we won't be in a recession; if you pick up this book in ten years, we most likely will be back in a recession. The economic environment you're in will determine where you will invest more, and in which asset classes. If you want to grow your money when the economy isn't doing well then cash is king. Interest rates are high now, which will benefit you to grow your money. But if the environment is on the upswing, then you have different options to invest your money; it all depends on the economic environment. To be an informed investor and empower your view of finance, you need to know the financial language. That begins with understanding asset classes.

In finance, you will hear people refer to "portfolios." I had someone say, "Like, is that an actual book?" The answer is no, a portfolio isn't a book. This is the term for your group of financial investments. Asset classes are also groups. They're a group of financial investments that includes cash, alternative assets, stocks, futures, and fixed-income investments. So if you have a group of investments, then you have an asset, or a portfolio.

There are many ways to invest, but first it's important to understand the two ways to look at investing strategies. There's investing for the short term, and there's investing for the long term. Anything over twelve months is considered a long-term investment, and anything less than twelve months is considered short-term. With a short-term investment, you plan to have your money wrapped up for a short time (for less than twelve months) before you expect a return. Long-term investments take a little bit longer to mature or show a return.

The name of the game is to have a diverse portfolio—to spread out your investments across different groups to increase your chances to grow your money. A diverse portfolio is important because you don't want to get too fixated on only one way to invest. Most people think that the only way to invest is through the stock market or through retirement accounts. When you look at asset classes, you open your mind to the many different categories in which you can invest your money and the many ways to grow your money.

Let's take a look at the five major asset classes:

▸ Alternative assets, which are usually physical assets like fine watches, real estate, collectible cars, art, and jewelry

▸ Stocks, which represent ownership of a piece of a publicly traded company

▸ Fixed-income investments such as government bonds and deposit certificates

▸ Cash, such as dollar bills, and cash equivalents such as savings accounts, retirement accounts, and 401(k)s

▸ Futures and other derivatives, which are contracts between two parties agreeing to buy and sell assets, usually commodities like gold, corn, wheat, or cows, at a future date

Reasons to Invest (or Not) in the Five Major Asset Classes

Keep in mind that this section is intended only to introduce you to asset classes for educational purposes, not to offer investment advice. The market is constantly in flux, and things change. As such, and as I always emphasize, there is no such thing as a low-risk or no-risk investment.

Asset Classes at a Glance

Asset Class	Includes	Why to Invest	Why Not to Invest
Alternative assets	Physical items like art, real estate, or luxury goods	People who invest in alternative assets typically have more money to play with. These assets often outperform the S&P 500 and typically perform better in a recession.	The gain in the value of alternative assets depends on resale value and demand.
Stocks (equities)	A piece or share of ownership of a company	Investing in a well-researched and well-chosen stock can deliver a great return. This strategy is called "buy low, sell high."	Neglecting to learn the market and do your research can make investing money in stock a high-risk gamble. Your return on investment depends on the ups and downs of the market, which is constantly moving ("market volatility").
Fixed-income investments	Government bonds, deposit certificates	Although there's no such thing as a completely low-risk investment, fixed-income investments come closest. They are considered low-risk, long-term investments.	Making money on a fixed-income investment takes a long time as you wait for the bonds to mature, and the value of your investment at maturity can depend on the state of the market when you cash in your bonds.
Cash and cash equivalents	Cash, savings accounts, retirement accounts, 401(k)s	Cash is king. With this asset, if you need cash in an emergency, you have access to it.	Savings accounts gain little interest, and your money isn't growing with inflation.
Futures and other derivatives	Futures are contracts to buy and sell commodities—gold, farm animals, wheat, corn, etc.—at an agreed-upon time in the future.	These assets are typically used for short-term investing.	Most financial advisers would not advise a client to invest in futures because the process is very complicated.

Alternative Assets

One alternative asset is real estate—the heart of the American dream. That's how it's been packaged to us. Real estate is a longer-term investment and, for the most part, is a safe bet here in America. You're not going to buy property in 2022 for $100,000 and then sell it for $46,000 thirty years later. For the most part, real estate gains in value and is considered a low-risk investment for this reason.

Luxury items in this asset class, such as a Basquiat painting, a Chanel handbag, or even fine wine, are probably more for high-net-worth investors. For the most part, these assets are not going to lose their value but will appreciate over the course of many years. The benefit to this asset class is that it doesn't perform on par with how the stock market moves. Take trading in an index fund like the S&P 500. During August 2022, your return for the year if you invested in that index was −15.86 percent. Negative! If you invested in fine wine at the beginning of the year, your return would be close to 11.12 percent in August. This tells us that you are probably going to outperform the stock market. You're going to outperform with this asset class because if your items don't get destroyed and are physically safe, then they hold their value. Besides being considered low-risk and safe, alternative assets have the benefit of giving you returns that are way larger than what you would see in a mutual fund, in equities, or in cash.

Stocks

Investing in the stock market and choosing the sector of it to invest in are going to depend on how much money you have to invest in this asset class, as well as on your financial goals and your risk tolerance. You can invest in small-cap or large-cap companies; these terms refer to "market capitalization," or the total value of the company's stock, that is, how much these companies are valued at. Large-cap companies are valued at over $10 billion, and small-cap companies are valued at between $250 million and $2 billion. The difference is important because the companies you invest in will be grouped into different indexes depending on their size. The S&P 500 holds large-cap companies, and the Russell 2000, another index, holds small-cap companies. Your returns will vary depending on the sector of the stock market you invest in. Returns in some sectors are potentially larger than returns in other sectors depending on where things are with the stock market.

Besides coming in different sizes, stocks also do different things. Some stocks pay dividends, giving you passive monthly income. Other stocks don't generate dividends; you'll make money on this type only when you sell the stock. The way to make money is to buy stock at a low price and then sell it when it's hot and its value is high.

Here's a breakdown of important things to know about the stock markets and exchanges:

▸ *S&P 500:* The Standard & Poor's 500 is an index made up of the top five hundred largest publicly traded companies in the United States. You can invest in any stock, and in any index, but the S&P 500 is the stock market that most people trade in, and it's probably going to be your entry point into trading. But remember, with investing, nothing is ever set in stone.

▸ *The Nasdaq:* The National Association of Securities Dealers Automated Quotations is an online marketplace or exchange where you can buy and sell securities. The Nasdaq was created specifically to exchange electronic securities. You'll find tech stocks listed here. If you're a tech entrepreneur, you can have your company listed here at the time of your initial public offering (IPO). For example, Tesla is listed on the Nasdaq.

▸ *The Dow:* The Dow Jones Industrial Average is a stock market index that tracks the thirty most traded blue-chip companies in the United States. Blue-chip companies are nationally recognized and financially sound companies. They are known for being stable during economic downturns.

Did you know that the stock market has eleven different sectors? That means eleven different places to invest your money! Here are examples of the types of companies found in each sector:

▸ *Consumer discretionary:* Retail, luxury goods, and travel and leisure companies

▸ *Consumer services:* Media and entertainment companies, such as television, radio, social media, and wireless telecom networks

▸ *Consumer staples:* Food and beverage companies and companies that manufacture personal products, household goods, and other items that consumers absolutely need, like toilet paper

▸ *Energy:* Oil, natural gas, clean energy, and sustainable energy companies

▸ *Financials:* Banks, asset management companies, and financial brokers

▸ *Health care:* Health care services, biotech, insurance companies, and pharmaceuticals

▸ *Industrials:* Aerospace, defense, and machinery manufacturers

▸ *Information technology:* Tech companies involved in cloud computing, software and hardware companies, and the largest tech companies

▸ *Materials:* Manufacturers of construction materials and metals, paper manufacturers

▸ *Real estate:* Real estate companies, real estate management companies, real estate investment trusts

▸ *Utilities:* Water, gas, and electricity companies

Fixed-Income Investments

Treasuries are fixed-income investments. Backed by the US government, Treasuries, which include bills, bonds, notes, and corporate bonds, are safe. You gain a return on Treasuries according to the term and rate at which you purchased them. Bills are short-term—investments of less than twelve months. Notes can be issued at a fixed rate and for terms of two to ten years. US Treasury bonds are issued for terms of thirty years or more.

Because all Treasury investments are backed by the government, they're safe and considered low-risk or even literally no-risk. During economic downturns, Treasuries are more attractive because as interest rates rise Treasury rates usually rise too. When the economy is doing well, they are still a safe option, but you won't see returns as high as 4 percent but something closer to 1 or 2 percent.

Know that returns on fixed-income investments are going to be significantly lower than on investments in the S&P 500 over the course of ten years. The return on fixed-income investments can be around 3 percent. That's better than a savings account, but lower than the S&P, which can bring returns of around 9 percent. With fixed-income investments your money is safe and it's guaranteed, but again, they're not going to give you high returns. These investments are a low-risk way to park your money, grow your money, and keep your money safer than with other asset classes.

Certificates of deposit

Ever wonder how you can invest your money, grow your money, and build credit at the same time? Certificates of deposit, also known as CDs, do just that. CDs, another kind of savings account, are found at credit unions and banks. They work a bit like Treasuries in that you buy them at their face value. CDs are deposit accounts based on a "term" (another word for "time"). When you see your interest grow on your money depends on the term that you purchased the CD under—anywhere from three to sixty months.

For example, if you purchase a CD for three months with an interest rate of 3.5 percent, you have to hold the CD for three months to get back the initial value of what you purchased it for. Once the three months have passed, then you will see your purchase grow by 3.5 percent. Just like Treasuries, CDs generally have interest rates that are not so great when the economy and the market are in a good place, but rates rise when we are in an economic downturn. There are also some other pros and cons to CDs:

Pros: I like CDs as an option for people who are trying to build credit because they can take a loan out on the CD they purchased, ending up with a CD *and* a separate loan. You can take a loan out for the full value of the CD, park that loan money in an untouched account, and then pay back the loan in full by its term date—say in three months. Once that loan is paid back in full, your credit score will go up. So it's a win.

Cons: There are steep penalties to withdrawing money from your CD early (not from the loan). If you expect to need to touch that money before the term date, I would look into other investment options. Purchasing a CD may not be the best bet for you.

Cash and Cash Equivalents

Cash and cash equivalents like your savings account are what we call "liquid," which means that the cash is not caught up in investments. If you need your money, it's not going to take much time to get the money out of the account or investment. In a pinch, you have access to that cash.

Cash and cash equivalents are considered a low-risk investment. Putting money in your savings account is not going to give you a large percentage of interest on your dollar, but it is another low-risk, low-reward way to continue to grow your money. It's a better investment than stashing your bills in a piggy bank, which gives you zero interest. It's also best to have cash on hand when preparing for recession, and we can always expect that there will be another one.

Futures

Investing in futures is a way to profit short-term in the market. Most people investing in futures will go through a financial adviser, though most wealth managers and other professionals who help people with their investment strategy tend to tell people to stay away from options and futures because they're high-risk. It's true that futures are a slippery slope. I always ask, "You want to see your money grow?" but with futures I say, "So you want to see your money go!"

But in all seriousness, no asset class is completely risk-free. Again, you have to know what you're doing. All asset classes, whether alternative assets, stocks, fixed income, cash, or futures, can grow your money. Some are guaranteed, such as Treasuries, and are safe. Others can get a little wonky. Cryptocurrencies, for example, are high-risk but high-reward. Crypto can grow your money, but again, there's no guarantee that they will.

Futures are considered leverage trading, which is risky. But you can do it right, and if you do, you could get forty times what you put in. Futures are for investors who can take more risks, people who are willing to lose their money for the chance to trade in high-risk, high-reward futures. But for the vast majority of people, I as well as other advisers wouldn't even consider adding futures to your portfolio.

–9–

Planning for Retirement

It's fair to say that most young people are probably not focusing on or seriously planning for retirement, but they absolutely should. According to the Federal Reserve, younger adults, those ages eighteen to twenty-nine, are less likely than older adults to save for retirement or to feel like they're on track with their retirement savings. This is even more true for Black and Hispanic adults who have not yet reached retirement age.

It's important to understand that a lack of retirement savings contributes to the wealth gap. The NAACP attributes this lack to the fact that Black people in America have traditionally had lower salaries than their white counterparts owing to factors such as systemic racism. With a lower salary, it's harder to save. You need most of the money you're paid for your day-to-day and monthly expenses, but saving is not impossible. I watched my mom save and plan and prioritize with what money she had, so I know it can be done whether you're making $30,000 a year or $100,000.

Although it may seem far off, *it's important to start thinking about retirement now*. Later in your life you'll want to have that money to fall back on. It may be hard to think so long-term, especially if retirement is far in the future for you. But if you can understand the importance of saving and wrap your mind around the concept of having an emergency fund—liquid cash stored away to use when you really need it—then you can understand the concept of saving for retirement. It's essentially the same thing. Funding your retirement is something that you should always be thinking about for your future.

People retire for many different reasons. Look, some of us don't especially like to work. Some of us will retire because we need a change. According to the Federal Reserve, 49 percent of people surveyed said they retired because they wanted something else to do. Twenty-nine percent retired because of a health problem. So the reasons to retire aren't always about retiring in the traditional view of it as sitting back on a beach somewhere drinking a Mai Tai with your legs up. Maybe you're using that retirement money to create generational wealth by helping your child put a deposit down on their first home. Maybe further down the line you want to use that extra financial cushion to help your grandchild start a business. It's all savings, and what you want to do with your savings is completely up to you. If possible, though, it's savings that you really don't want to touch until later in your life.

Know that retirement isn't a destination but an ongoing financial journey. I grew up with my grandparents, who have always been financially responsible. In fact, everything that I know about personal finances comes from my mom and my grandparents; all of them have always been smart with money. My grandparents did what they were supposed to and definitely saved for retirement. But oddly enough, once they got to retirement, they realized that maybe they hadn't really thought ahead as much as they should have. It's like they completely forgot all the financial lessons they taught me and the rest of the family. I think they got to a place where they wanted to enjoy life and splurge. But now, after spending so much early in their retirement, they've already blown through their money.

My advice is to budget and plan and save for retirement and be among the 52 percent of older adults (age sixty-five and older), according to a 2022 Federal Reserve report, who feel like their retirement savings are on track. If you can, try to do what you can right now. But when you get to retirement age, when you get to your seventies, remember the importance of maintaining your financial wellness and keeping up your financial literacy.

You'll need to continue to budget and save. You can't just say, "Okay, now I'm seventy, I'm retired now, so I can just go crazy with money." No! You still have to support yourself through all of retirement, however long that is for you. You have to keep your financial foundation solid because otherwise you may need to go back to work. You probably don't want to be doing that during your later years, when you just want to enjoy life. So hopefully, in building this foundation now, you'll continue to manage your money responsibly once you get to that milestone. *If you master the habits I'm teaching you in this book about financial wellness, they will serve you when you're twenty, when you're seventy, and when you're one hundred years old.*

Start Budgeting, Saving, and Investing for Retirement Now

Saving for retirement should start as soon as you want to start budgeting and saving. One of the reasons why I was crazy about saving 80 percent of my income was knowing that a percentage of that would go toward my retirement. What percentage goes toward retirement is up to you. Some financial experts will tell you that you should save 15 percent of your pretax income each year. That may not be realistic for you.

A good approach to retirement savings is to follow the 50:30:20 rule that we talked about in chapter 4. Your retirement savings should come out of the 20 percent you put aside for savings. I want to make it clear that not all of that 20 percent set aside for savings should go toward retirement but rather a percentage of it. It could be 5 percent or 10 percent of that 20 percent, with the rest of your savings budget of 20 percent of your income going toward regular savings, such as your emergency fund. Again, it's completely up to you, and what makes sense to you for your planning and your goals. If, for example, you want to retire young, you may want to build up your retirement funds by being more aggressive with your savings and investing and . . . well, you would obviously also need a really good job!

I'm not asking you to have enough money in the bank to support yourself and fund your kid's life for the next forty years, although it's not necessarily unrealistic. I'm sure some people have been in a financial situation to do that and have done it, but I think the vast majority of those of you reading this book are probably not going to be able to do that. Your finances are going to need lifelong management. And the sooner you start thinking and planning for the long term, the better off you'll be in the future.

Questions to Ask Yourself

Do I like to work?

Do I love my job?

Do I want to still be working in my thirties? Forties? Fifties? Sixties? Seventies?

Will I have enough money if I have to stop working unexpectedly, like for health reasons or to care for an aging parent?

Your honest answers to these questions may motivate you to start saving and investing for your future now, knowing that your sacrifices today will set you up for the future. For example, if you don't like to work, if you don't like your job, then planning for retirement means putting money toward the goal of knowing there'll be a day when you can take a break and do something that really lights your soul.

Not everybody wants to stop working. Maybe you're already doing something that lights you up, something that feels like your purpose, or your passion. For you, work is not going to feel like work and you'll continue to want to do it, maybe even well into your senior years. We have so many examples of that in Hollywood—actors Denzel Washington and Whoopi Goldberg, for example, have worked past the typical retirement age. If you're fortunate enough to find what feels like your purpose, that job or career or business that lights you up, and you're willing to continue to work all the way through to what people think of as retirement age, then you have found your place. On the other hand, it's not a terrible thing if you have not found that purpose or passion.

Some people love their job, but is it their absolute passion? No. They want to stop working eventually, and that's also okay. So it's always about doing what is right for you and knowing that there's no wrong or right answer. *Imagine having the financial freedom to really choose to work or not.*

How Do You Want to Live Later in Your Life?

I know when you're young it's hard to wrap your mind around these thoughts. I'm in my twenties, so I can't say what my life is going to be like when I'm seventy. But planning starts with vision, and vision starts the journey. You can even make a vision board to support this conversation.

Making a vision board

Cut out images from magazines, catalogs, and newspapers to make a collage that represents your plans, dreams, and goals for your life. If one day you want to own a vineyard and produce your own private-label wine, you could cut out an image of a wineglass or a sunny vineyard and paste it to your vision board. Maybe you could add a picture of the dog breed you always wanted. Or a car that will look good on you when you're gray.

Using a vision board to start imagining your best life will help keep you on track when you're planning for your future, and it will remind you why you're setting aside that retirement money. Why you're not spending it all right this minute. Because you have plans, and they look good!

Ask yourself the following questions about retirement:

What do you want your life to be like when you reach the typical retirement age?

How much money will you need to live off each year if you're not working?

Where do you want to live? In a retirement home? In a house by the beach? In a condo in the city? Maybe you want two homes?

What do you want to do with your time when you're older?

Do you care about having enough savings to do something like buy a boat and sail up the coast?

Do you want to start a small business, such as a vegan ice cream shop?

Asking questions like these can help you start putting these things in place for yourself right now, no matter what age you are. Whatever your vision of your future, there's going to be a time when you'll need to have the resources to take care of yourself and to live your best life.

Maybe your retirement savings can help you with unexpected life changes. Maybe you'll need that extra cushion to help take care of your parents. I'm always looking at my finances over the long term because I'll need to care for my brother. If you just live for the now, you're missing the opportunity to set yourself up for long-term wealth, support, and wellness, because wellness takes resources.

No matter what age you are now, you don't want to be older and worried about how to care for yourself or your family. You don't ever want to just burn through your money and live for the moment, spending irresponsibly, because you're going to need that money at some point. You're going to have to make a plan, whether that's a self-directed retirement savings plan (meaning you are the one making the decisions about your money) or parking your money in a traditional retirement plan such as a 401(k) or Roth IRA.

Why I Am Not a Fan of Retirement Accounts

Did you know that 401(k)s were not originally meant to be used as retirement accounts? Historically in the United States a proper retirement account was a solid pension plan: the employer would contribute regularly to this fund, which was set aside to fund the employee's retirement income. In the United States today, however, employers rarely offer a pension plan.

More and more often we're expected to manage our own retirement funds, using popular kinds of retirement accounts like 401(k) and IRA accounts. I'll explain why I'm not a fan of these accounts.

Most retirement accounts are invested in mutual funds by an active account manager.

Where you choose to put your retirement savings is completely up to you. Again, I'm not a fan of traditional retirement accounts, such as a 401(k) or Roth IRA. Typically, they're set up so that you're putting your money into mutual funds. Most workplace 401(k)s also have contribution limits, as well as different income limits that you'll need to look into. While a 401(k) does help you save money toward retirement, there are limits to the amount of money you can put into this kind of account.

A mutual fund is one in which your money is actively managed by an actual person, unlike an index fund, in which your money is passively managed. Using algorithms, index funds consistently track the largest five hundred companies on the S&P 500. Since they literally just follow what the S&P 500 is doing, index funds don't involve a human investing money on your behalf, whereas a lot of retirement accounts have a fund manager.

A fund manager is a professional who is actively investing your money. With each managed fund, your risk and gains depend on the assets in which the fund manager decides to invest. If they're not so great at their job, you can lose some of your hard-earned retirement money. According to CNBC, actively managed funds underperformed in 2021, following a similar long-term trend. Managed accounts have always performed worse than other accounts.

Most retirement accounts have costly fees.

When you're choosing a retirement account, pay attention to the associated fees. How much will you be charged in fees just to park your money? Look, I don't like the fees associated with retirement accounts. When I broke it down by numbers, I found that people pay significantly higher fees for actively managed accounts than for passive accounts.

For example, if I put my money into the S&P 500, I'm paying around 0.09 percent in fees. If I open up a brokerage account on Robinhood, I don't have to pay any commission or fees, for the most part, but if I do the fees will come to about 0.09 percent. So these fees are very low. On the other hand, if I put my money into a mutual fund, I'm paying fees that average 0.82 percent. That's a big difference in fees. You want to pay that 0.09 percent, not 0.82 percent, right? We always want to pay lower fees, to have less money being taken from us.

It's important to wrap your mind around what this means for

your hard-earned long-term savings, since these percentages are so jarring. Let's break them down into actual numbers. Let's say you invest $1,000 annually in the S&P 500. So each year, over the course of thirty years, you're adding $1,000. Getting a 7 percent return on your investment, you will make $99,000 over thirty years. If you put $1,000 annually into mutual funds for thirty years at 7 percent interest, you're going to get a return of $86,000. We're talking a difference in earnings between index funds and mutual funds of $13,000. That's a lot of money! It's more than I made my first year working on the New York Stock Exchange.

Now let's look at the fees associated with these gains. That 0.09 percent in fees over thirty years of putting money into an S&P 500 account is going to look like a total of $1,800. That's what I will pay on fees by putting my money in an index fund, just using my little account online. If you put your money into a mutual fund, the fees over thirty years at 0.82 percent are going to look like $15,600. So you're really not even making that $86,000, because you have to subtract the $15,600 you're paying in fees. Your gains will look more like $70,400 than the $86,000 you may have expected.

Your money is locked away in a retirement account.

The issue I have with most 401(k) retirement accounts is that you can't withdraw your money before you're fifty-nine and a half years old. If you're doing well financially, it is less likely that you'll need to make withdrawals. The Federal Reserve found that 12 percent of people with a retirement account balance of less than $50,000 borrowed from or cashed out these retirement accounts before they could do so without penalty. These were lower-income people who may have found themselves in need of that money.

In fact, when people are in financial hardships, retirement accounts are one of the first places that they tap into their money. This is the very last place you should go. I understand the why, I empathize with the why. People typically have a healthy sum of cash stored there. During the pandemic, the CARES Act in the US allowed for people to take out up to $100,000, with no penalties, from their retirement account but they had to pay that money back three years later. In 2020 during the pandemic, we were definitely in the era of free money. And we are now in 2023 seeing the firsthand consequences of doing so. The impulse to dip into that money was there. In fact, Fidelity Investments, the largest provider of 401(k) plans in the US, showed that more than 700,000 people took from their 401(k)s or other retirement plans. And more than 18,000 people asked for the full $100,000 amount.

I want to say it again: Tapping into a retirement account should be a *last* resort. Exhaust your other options. If you are fortunate enough to own a home, I would suggest you take out a home equity line of credit, maybe taking out another bank loan. Potentially use credit cards with 0 percent interest on purchases.

Unfortunately, if you need to withdraw that money before you're fifty-nine and a half, you incur a 10 percent tax penalty and also have to pay income tax on any amount you withdraw. There are exceptions to this rule. Sometimes you can withdraw money for certain hardships; you'll still have to pay the 10 percent early withdrawal fee, but you may be able to avoid paying income tax on the amount you take out. Still, if you just put that money into your own brokerage account instead of a retirement fund, you wouldn't have to pay those taxes and penalties for withdrawing your money.

The main lesson that we need to understand when planning for our future is that even though we can plan to the best of our ability so that we won't need our money until we're fifty-nine and a half years old, life sometimes happens, especially to people who are struggling financially. In those moments when you need access to your funds, you don't want your money locked up.

Look, imagine you put $20,000 over the course of your life into a mutual fund, and you can't touch that money without being penalized; you're not going to be happy about that. Like most people, you may need to access that money before retirement, especially if you want to reach certain lifestyle milestones, whether it's buying a house or getting married. These are some of the big moments in your life when you may need to have large sums of money. This is when you need access to your money. I'm by no means advocating that you deplete your retirement or savings accounts to cover these milestone expenses. But the money you've set aside for retirement can also be a cushion when you just need a little extra money that your savings account doesn't cover.

Another issue is that tax is deferred on many retirement accounts. What many of us don't realize is that most of us are not going to be making the same money at twenty-one as we are at fifty. Right. Our income will have scaled throughout our career. And so, when you're fifty years old and in a higher tax bracket, you actually will owe more in taxes when you go to withdraw that money than you would have when you started the account.

Planning for Retirement by Investing in Long-Term, Low-Risk Assets

There is absolutely a need to have a retirement account. It's to give you that cushion to fund your life after work. And we see that most governments around the world, people around the world, are trying to unlock that secret formula on how to do so. The best advice that I have to give to everyone is to take matters into your own hands. Please don't count solely on programs your country gives you to sustain your retirement.

We need to get empowered to manage our money, especially our retirement funds. We can think outside the box when it comes to retirement. We don't always have to agree with what is being presented to us as retirement plans. The more we know about money and finances, the more empowered we are. This is so important for those of us who are not used to managing and thinking, or even talking, about money. Minorities, women, young people. We have to start these conversations now.

Finances are not just for one group of people, even if finances have been traditionally dominated by one group. It is time that we changed that dynamic. According to the Federal Reserve, *men are twice as likely (65 percent) as women (33 percent) to feel comfortable managing their own retirement savings.* Women also reported less financial literacy and less comfort in managing retirement savings. This is not what we want. I'd like everyone to feel empowered enough to manage their own retirement savings. This takes some confidence, planning, and know-how.

I'm a huge proponent of planning for your future by investing your money in assets that are long-term, assets that are low-risk, and assets that are safer than traditional retirement accounts such as the 401(k), the IRA, and the Roth IRA. The truth is that when you go to get your money out of a mutual fund, depending on the market at that time, and accounting for the fees associated with retirement accounts and the 10 percent penalty and taxes owed if you withdrew your money before you were fifty-nine and a half, maybe it turns out not to have been worth it. That's why I want to empower you to save and grow your money without locking it up somewhere. You can invest in other assets that may return more of your money to you when it comes time to get that money out.

As I've said, I'm not a huge fan of traditional retirement accounts. I know that stance might be controversial, but look, I'm writing this book in the belief that financial decisions are personal. You have to do your own research to make the informed decisions that are best for your own personal circumstances.

So, in general, you want to invest and grow your money by putting it in absolutely safe conservative vehicles such as Treasuries, bonds, and high-yield savings accounts. You want to be parking your money where you know for sure that it's going to grow interest, but without losing its value and with the least number of penalties and fees possible.

You don't have to be an American citizen to invest in Treasuries, bonds, or index funds.

Investments I Recommend for Retirement

▸ Treasuries

▸ CDs

▸ Bonds

▸ High-yield savings accounts

▸ Index funds (which carry no guarantees but are cheaper than mutual funds because of lower fees)

Career Advice

Be Open to Possibilities

I didn't choose the New York Stock Exchange;
the New York Stock Exchange chose me.

Wherever you may be on your career journey, whether you're an intern or an executive, know that when you remain open to all the exciting possibilities to share your talents and gifts, that's when the magic happens. Whatever that looks like for you, whether you're working a nine-to-five job, starting a brick-and-mortar business, or looking to fund your tech startup, I really do believe that you get back what you put in, even if in the end it looks different than what you expected. Stay open to learning, exploring, and growing, and stay open to different opportunities. The sky really is the limit.

You Don't Need to Find Your Purpose Right Away

I don't want anyone to think that they need to find their passion, their purpose, today. Those of you who do find your passion and purpose today, realize that may change in ten years and that's okay. You can do what feels good for you in the moment. My work, for example, is currently centered on finances. At this moment in time, I truly love finance, and I will continue to love finance until I love doing something else. And remember, I didn't study finance in school; my studies were in architectural engineering. My journey, with all of its twists and turns and bumps in the road, finally led me to finance because I wanted something more for myself and I was open to the possibilities.

When it comes to choosing a career path, I know how hard it can be to find your way. It can take a while for some people to figure out what they want to do, while others seem to know right away. Sometimes success can happen fast, or things can take longer for other people, and that's okay. Either way, you have to want that success, that career, for yourself, and you have to be willing to do the work, and you need the strength to keep trying.

I don't want anyone to be too hard on themselves when they're trying to find out what they're going to do. Not everyone knows straight away what career they'll go into. I don't want you to be down on yourself if you're not where you want to be yet, if you haven't reached that place you thought you'd be by now. Careers take time, and all of us are always a work in progress. Even the people at the top keep striving. That's how they got there in the first place, knowing that it's always a journey, not a destination.

Believe in Yourself and Your Values

When you're looking for your career path, for the ways you can really shine, you first and foremost must believe that you will eventually find your ideal occupation. That's the first step—believing that you can. Believing that you will eventually find the career that lights you up, that you will find the work that aligns with your spirit. That place, occupation, or position in which you feel valued and can truly shine will come to you eventually if you are unwilling to settle for less than you envision for yourself.

Unlock a Roadmap with Journaling

Find a quiet place to reflect and unwind. Look at yourself in the mirror and ask yourself the following questions. Then write down your honest answers. Know that they may change as you change and grow. But your answers may offer some insight into a few areas that you may want to pursue for now:

What do you like to do for fun?

What makes you smile?

What would you love to be paid to do?

What kind of things do you do for free?

Do you love doing your friends' hair? Grooming your dog? Cooking for friends?

Is there a problem in the world that you would love to solve?

Who are you jealous of?

What would it say about you if you appeared on the cover of a magazine?

If children make you smile, maybe you want to open a day care center, become a teacher, or write children's books. If you love cooking, maybe you want to quit your job as a lawyer and open a restaurant, take a food truck on the road, or become a chef. If you love brushing your dog's hair, maybe starting a pet grooming franchise would light up your purpose?

Remember You Have Choices and Leverage

If you ever find yourself feeling undervalued in your job or in your organization, know that people have so much more leverage nowadays. Especially in these pandemic and post-pandemic times, it's a job-seekers' market, and people are speaking up and organizing and pushing back on issues such as the ability to work remotely. People can get exactly what they want, and if their company isn't giving it to them, they're putting together an exit strategy and looking to join an organization that's more aligned with their values and ethics and offers the benefits and salary they're seeking.

Workers are taking back a lot of power and saying, "I'm going to work, I'm going to find my purpose, I'm going to work in an environment that feels good to me." They're letting go of what doesn't serve them and moving on to get what they want, whether that's working remotely, receiving paid paternity leave, or speaking out online against unfair company policies. These are all ways in which workers are reclaiming their power.

Don't Compare Your Career to Other People's Careers

It's human nature to want to measure our careers against what other people are doing. Again, some people are very successful when they're young and seem to have it all figured out on day one. For other people, the journey may take a little longer. Some people finish school in four years, and some take a little longer because of setbacks or personal issues. It's all good—just keep going at your own pace.

A comparing and contrasting mindset is never helpful and not even healthy. The only way comparison adds value is if it lights a competitive fire in you. Otherwise, comparisons are mostly counterproductive, especially if you're just using them to beat yourself up and fall into a "poor me" attitude. That rarely gets you to a place of empowerment and progress. I think everyone's timeline is different, and your milestones are exactly where they're meant to be for you individually at any specific time. Don't get too caught up in thinking, like, "Oh, this person is so much further ahead," because then you're really getting into the self-sabotage talk. Creating an energetically negative vibe isn't going to motivate you or push you forward. If anything, it's going to depress you and hold you back.

Be grateful and try to be enriched in knowing that a successful person you know got there. You can use that as inspiration. Now you know that it is possible to get there and that you'll get there as well if you do some of the same things. *Another person's success can be your success.* You can mirror them. You can feel good about where they're at. You can even study their success and see if you can crack their code. What did this person do to get where they are? Are you willing to do the same? If not, then the comparison is just a waste of time and a distraction from your own goals.

Bring High Vibes to Your Work

Pay attention to the energy that you bring to your work. Are you bringing a negative vibe to your work because maybe you're feeling a bit overworked, undervalued, or disgruntled? If you're feeling stuck in a position, or in a business that you don't love, being negative is not going to help you. It's not going to make your management or your organization look at you positively. Is your negative attitude going to set you up for a promotion? Probably not. Remember that we get back what we put in, and bringing a negative attitude to work is not how you get the things that you may want for yourself. It's just not.

A positive attitude comes from knowing that you are in control of your career, education level, skills building, and additional training. You are in control of your career destiny. Positive progress begins and ends with the right attitude. Knowing that things can work out in the end when you take positive steps toward being your best self will put you in a better mindset to get what you want within the organization. A positive attitude will also make you confident that you can look elsewhere at companies that may offer more opportunities for your career growth. Being miserable is just never a good look.

When you do find yourself in a funk, it's okay. Your feelings are a clue. But that doesn't mean that you should stay in a funk. Stop using excuses. Take it head-on. You have the ability at any moment to change your life circumstances. And this advice isn't just some old hippie way of thinking. This is real. If you lead with your intuition and have made an affirmation that you truly believe in, then you already have the right foundation.

Let Positive Thoughts Lead to Positive Results

Transforming your life starts with believing in the process, in yourself, and in your power. If you can't see it for yourself, who else is going to see it for you? You may get that job, and you may get that meeting that you wanted, and you may get the chance to network with the right people, but guess what? If you show up with the wrong attitude, the wrong vibe, if you bring a negativity to those opportunities, then ultimately they may end up crumbling because you didn't perform well. You allowed the negative self-talk to start going through your thoughts. Your body language isn't good. All of this gets in the way of acing that interview, or presenting that pitch, or securing that funding, because you let negativity take away from your ability to perform well.

Vibrationally, you want to be in a place where you are happy and you believe it. You can see it. And I'm not talking about a fake happiness. I don't want you to have the unhealthy kind of happy feelings. Your feelings are valid, and you should feel them. Allow yourself to feel all the feelings, with enough time and space to feel whatever those emotions are. Maybe it's one day, maybe it's a few hours. It should not be more than twenty-four hours. Then you have to start thinking about changing your circumstances.

What you don't want is to find yourself in a place where you have the same narrative and the same words coming into your head on cycle, coming in on repeat, and you're wondering why you're not getting further in your career. You're wondering why you're not meeting the right people. You're wondering why you're not getting the job guarantee. It's all about the vibration that you're bringing to the universe. It's all about how you are carrying yourself moment by moment, day by day. Yeah, you can definitely complain, you're human. We all complain sometimes. Your emotions are valid, but you can't consistently have that "woe is me" mentality turned on. It won't serve you. It isn't coming from a place of power.

Ask Yourself: "How Do I Move Forward?"

Okay, you gave yourself that time and space to feel your feelings. Now ask yourself, "How do I move forward?" You can start your day by doing your mirror work, starting with this affirmation: "I have the power to change this situation."

Then you can use journaling to build your strategy. Start by being patient with yourself, but also being real with yourself. Answer these questions honestly:

Have I tried all the avenues that I want to?

Have I asked for resources within my organization?

Have I actually been out doing the work?

Have I reached out to other people who can help me so that I don't feel like I have to do this all on my own?

Ask for help.

I'm a person who dislikes asking for help from other people. I always want to do it all by myself. I feel like I need to do everything by myself and almost feel ashamed to ask people for help, whether it's asking someone to introduce me to someone else, asking for help to grow my business, asking for networking opportunities, or asking about job openings. I've learned, though, that, sure, you can do it by yourself—people do claim to have done it all themselves—but it's so much harder to do by yourself than it is to ask for help. You don't have to be prideful. More likely than not, that person you see on top got there by asking for help.

One of the things I do in my business is public speaking. My speeches didn't get better until I started rehearsing my speeches with my mother and recording them and playing them back for others so I could hear feedback. My speeches weren't as great before then because I was afraid to ask for help and just assumed I had to do everything on my own.

It is okay to go to your people for help. Go to people who are going to be allies. People who can really help you and you trust well enough to review and onboard ideas with. People who can give you constructive feedback. Choose wisely when asking others for help. Would you go to one of your seniors at work who hasn't been supportive of you and often shuts down your ideas and ask them for help? Probably not. Would you go to your hairstylist and ask about your business? Maybe. If your hairstylist owns the salon or has a very lucrative business, they may be a good person to consult.

The point is to ask for help from people whom you can trust, who are safe, who have good intentions for you, and who want you to do well. Not everybody is going to be a safe space. You'll have to take time to determine who's trustworthy and who's qualified to help you or give you constructive feedback. To find out if you can trust someone, you have to extend yourself by asking questions that will show you whether it's safe to ask that person for help. Also consider talking to the people you admire. Do you know someone who's really got it together? Maybe it's time to ask her how she did it.

---

*Not everyone you approach will help you,
and that's okay. It still doesn't hurt to ask.*

Even with where I am today in my career, I can still get super-disappointed when I build people up in my head, and I'm thinking like, *Okay, I'm going to go ask how to get where they are now.* And then it's shocking when people are not helpful. They don't want to help. They had no interest in helping. And so I've just had to learn that a response like that has nothing to do with me. Still, it is hard in real time.

I'm sharing this to say that when asking for help in your career, definitely keep in mind that you don't want to build other people up in your head. Go ahead and ask, but protect your feelings, curb your expectations, and then be pleasantly surprised if it works out well. Because sometimes we have this whole scenario thought out, and we're really excited to reach out to someone we admire, and it literally happens 180 degrees different from how we envisioned it going.

Do it because you love it.

Pursue the career goals that are right for you. Pursue this path because you're called to it. Pursue it because you love it. Some of the biggest game-changers and disruptors throughout history were hidden figures, people who didn't get the recognition but still moved forward, still innovated, still did what they loved. When you do what's right for you, you never know your true impact on the world. Sometimes it's as simple as serving someone coffee with a smile. If you're looking for validation, for the awards, for the fame and accolades, that's your choice, but know that it's not always about being recognized. It's about your passion and your mission and your goals. No one else has to understand your goals, validate them, or reward your efforts.

In real time I just watched the Primetime Emmy Awards. I'm sure all the nominees would have loved to win, but the truth is that not everyone was going to win an Emmy. What was more important was how passionate each nominee was about the projects they worked on, their dedication to creating the stories that they told.

I would hope that your heart is in your work, that you're doing it for the love and not the accolades, because sometimes someone else gets the award and that's okay. It shouldn't stop you from pursuing your goals, passions, and dreams. You can get awards in a number of different industries, like Employee of the Month. Sometimes that looks great, that motivates you, but if you don't get that award, it doesn't mean that you're not valuable. It doesn't mean that your work isn't important. If you're working for yourself, you have to know that you're making a difference and that your business is valuable, in spite of how many other entrepreneurs there are. Your business is adding value to people's lives, even if you don't get the public recognition.

A step in the right direction is having that curiosity and remembering that career success is a process. When you know the importance of having fun with your career and you're vibrationally in a good place, things are going to eventually work out the way they're meant to. Don't put unnecessary emotional pressure on yourself. Don't pressure yourself to fit a certain mold by a certain time. Don't obsess about doing certain things by a certain age. That leads to a negative vibe, where you're beating yourself up unnecessarily. Negative self-talk rarely leads to progress.

When people don't meet the metrics or reach the milestones they set for themselves, sometimes I see them easily spiraling into a negative space. Always know that every defeat, every setback, every detour is meant to point you in the right direction.

A certain level of stress is necessary to succeed. If I'm being honest, every time in my life when I had a breakthrough, that happened for me because I put some things into motion. I was doing the work, and then I kind of just let go. I allowed myself to really trust in the universe. I made that intention, and I knew that it was going to work out. In those magical moments I just didn't put a high level of stress on it.

I know that, when I am vibrationally in a good place in my life, it's a time when I'm really trying not to control the outcome. I don't put the pressure of a timeline on my goals. I'm not saying, "I need to have this by this date," because that's never what ends up happening. It's like a push-and-pull kind of process: trying to find a healthy balance between stressing certain things and not stressing *about* them at all.

Be open. Be curious. Be flexible. Be fun.
Enjoy the journey. Enjoy the process. Do the work.
Set the intention, then let go . . .

As you're building your career and trying to lean energetically into a positive vibration, you can self-check with a barometer that helps you answer the question: "Am I in a positive vibration?"

How can you check to see if you're vibrationally in a good place? Take a look at this scale:

1 ☺	2	3	4	5
Opportunities and helpful people are attracted to me left and right.	I have a strong sense of purpose.	I'm filled with energy and joy and curiosity for my work.	I'm feeling secure and happy at work.	I feel insecure.
6	**7**	**8**	**9**	**10 ☹**
I'm feeling jealous of others at work. I try to sabotage their efforts.	I feel frustrated. I don't have what I need.	I feel angry all the time.	My work is making me feel physically sick and tired. I find myself complaining out loud.	I feel hopeless, stuck, and trapped in my job and my life. Things will never change.

Your feelings are valid.

You are going to find that where you stand on that scale can change from day to day. It's okay if you find yourself closer to 10 than 1. Your hope is just to not stay in that place for too long. Allow yourself space for your feelings, remembering that your emotions are valid. You're human.

Sometimes your feelings are cues that maybe it's time for a change, but it's unrealistic to think that you can go from 10 to 1 quickly, like in a day. It takes time to check in with yourself, survey the situation, and figure out how to move closer to a happier place in your day-to-day. I don't want to say that you have to have that hippie attitude of being positive every day or thinking you need to move through the scale quickly. It's unrealistic to think you need to go from angry to happy in a day.

It's good to feel your emotions. Check in on your feelings right where you are. If those emotions feel good, safe, and healthy, then that's good. Sometimes, though, it's also healthy to be angry, or worried, or frustrated. It's okay to feel stuck in a job, for example, if your job offers no room for career growth or promotion. It's healthy to notice that you're complaining at work more than usual, or that part of your job that once made you happy now feels like a painful chore. It can be helpful to ask yourself why you're suddenly angry, jealous of co-workers, or having a migraine headache every day. Pay attention to the way your body feels.

If your attitude is skewing more negative, use that emotional cue to plot a strategy that can bring things more into alignment with what you truly need in your career. After checking in on your attitude, you then want to figure out how to get from that level 8 of feeling angry to that level 4 of feeling happy with your work and experiencing the satisfaction of truly enjoying what you're working on.

To get back to being in a good vibrational place, you want to start scaling up that list. The more that you're in a good vibrational space, *the more that energy attracts positive things to you.* You will start feeling like things are going in a more positive direction and finding answers to problems that didn't even seem like they had solutions.

When you feel down or confused, or when things feel unclear, there are different things you can do to get unstuck. Maybe it's meditating for you, or maybe it's working out. Working out is very therapeutic because of how the mind-body connection works. Maybe for you getting unstuck is doing whatever it is that makes you feel your best and able to connect with your true self, whether that's dancing to your favorite song or finding the time to just do nothing. I'm a huge fan of vacations and sick days. If your employer gives you paid time off, take a day or two and don't feel guilty about it. Downtime is so important when you use it to pause and really take time to just reflect on what's going on with your headspace at the moment.

To reset your vibration try:

Taking a long walk with your dog (if you have one) or by
   yourself

Listening to a meditation

Taking a yoga or Pilates class

Going for a jog

Having a staycation

Doing nothing—just pausing

Taking a warm bath or shower

Basking in a hot tub

Working out at home or in the gym

Going to the park to put your bare feet in the grass or sit
   beneath a tree

Sitting by water—a river, lake, ocean, or pond

Saying a few affirmations

Doing some mirror work

Writing in your journal

Dancing to five of your favorite songs

Getting therapy

Taking a vacation

It's really about getting clear, creating the space to connect with your emotions, and then taking the time to clear away the emotions that aren't serving you.

A lot of self-help books are all about the power of positive thinking, and it's true that there is power in positive thinking. And the goal is to get to that positive place in your life, in your career. But to get there you have to be real about it. Look, work can be hard, and building a career isn't easy. If it was, everyone would be a success. So feel all those feelings, even the negative ones. Feel them for a little while, and then come up with a plan. You never want to stay in the "poor me" space. You don't want to bring that energy with you to your work, and it doesn't get you anywhere you want to go.

– 11 –

Entrepreneur Dos and Don'ts

If you have a bad relationship with money and your personal finances, then you're going to have a bad relationship with money when it comes to your business finances as well. Personal and professional relationships with money go hand in hand. But if you can manage your personal budget and build up your own savings, *there's a 90 percent chance you can do it in your professional role as well*.

This chapter gives you a quick rundown of a few of my entrepreneurial dos and don'ts:

Don't Impulse-Spend Business Income

When I first started making money, I would get my paychecks and then write out a check to my mom, who would never cash it. Then, after 180 days, the money would go right back into my account. This routine ensured that the money was not being spent for 180 days because I didn't have access to it.

We talked about this earlier in the book. How do you know if you're impulse-spending? If you do something like I did to make your money inaccessible for 180 days and find that you're still thinking about spending that money after 180 days have passed, then it's safe to say that is money that you really wanted to spend.

If you really need to impulse-spend and are financially re-sponsible, then buy the item. Sometimes I think I really want to buy something and then I bring the item home. And I wait. If I'm not reaching for the item within the return policy window, then it's not something that I actually need and I'll return it. Our brains are funny, and sometimes we just need to be in possession of things. But that doesn't mean we need it.

Do Spend Beneath Your Means

If you're always living marginally lower than what your income would fund, or running your business at a level lower than what it's bringing in, then you will always have a surplus of money. Seems simple, right?

For example, if your business is bringing in $1 million a year of revenue, you should aim to cover your expenses as if your revenues bring in only $200,000 a year. You should also aim not to use up all of your money in your personal life. If your salary is $60,000 a year after taxes, you really shouldn't live off of the full post-tax $60,000 salary. However crazy it sounds, try to live off of just $40,000. The point is that you always want to have extra money in reserve. The way to do that is to live and spend beneath your means, whether that's business or personal.

Do Pay Your Taxes!

Of course you should pay your taxes. Not paying taxes on your money as an entrepreneur lands a ton of people in financial trouble. We read about it in the news, especially when it's a celebrity who owes the IRS. Living beneath your means is all the more important when you own a business, because you're going to owe taxes. You may be able to reduce the amount you owe through tax loopholes, but we're not going to get into that. My only advice here is to hire a professional accountant to help you with that.

Living beneath your means when running a business works the same way as in your personal life. So, if your revenue is $100,000, you want to try to work with only $20,000. That way, you'll have 80 percent of your money free to go toward expenses such as taxes. Now, keep in mind that your tax bill won't be that high. At least, I seriously hope that's never the case! Just make sure you have enough money around to cover these things.

Do Make a Business Budget

Most of the fundamental principles of personal financial literacy laid out in this book can be applied to business as well. As a foundation, don't forget about the 50:30:20 rule when it comes to personal finances. This same rule works when you're organizing your business budget.

A Basic Business Budget

▸ The 20 percent goes to the future of your business so that you have a savings cushion—the reserves on hand to use on a rainy day.

▸ The 50 percent is for your business overhead, covering operation costs, employees' salaries, and whatever other expenses come up in running your business. I use 50 percent of my business budget for overhead a little differently because my brand is my business; the only people I have to pay out money to are the people on my team. I usually pay my team first.

▸ The 30 percent goes toward your "wants." Maybe you're looking to scale and grow your business. Maybe your business is a retail storefront. Maybe you would really like to hire additional workers. This 30 percent is for investing in whatever your wants are that are going to help your business scale and grow.

Do Get Past Those First Six Months

Understand that most businesses don't do well. Most businesses fail within the first six months of being created. Knowing this just comes with the territory. So if your business is doing well after the seventh month, use that initial success as an affirmation that your business will be just fine. At this point, you have survived the hardest part.

Do Know When to Take the Leap

If you are just beginning your career as an entrepreneur and still have a normal payroll job, then I would wait until you are confidently in a place where you can sustain yourself through your business before you take the leap of quitting your job and pursuing your business full-time. Now, I say that knowing that I myself didn't do that, but know that taking that leap really soon often doesn't work. You have to know where you stand first.

What it comes down to is knowing who you are and if you'll be okay taking this risk. I was making $12,000 a year when I took

the leap and said, "You know what? I'm going to be an entrepreneur!" That transition period caused me a lot of anxiety. I was
doing a few speaking engagements and had only about $10,000
in my bank account. It was scary. But you know, all I could do was
continue to hustle and grow and scale my business.

Like I always say, you have to figure out what makes the most
sense for you and only you. It may not make the most sense to
just leave your company right now. Or it may feel right to say,
"I'm just going to do it because I have an FU fund and I know
I'll be just fine." Ultimately, whether it makes more sense for
you to quit your job and start a business or wait until your
business has gotten to a place where you can sustain yourself is
a question that only you can answer for yourself.

Do Be Open to Change

I don't think you need to know what your true calling is in life
before you start your first business. I think starting your first business is more about being open and curious and flexible, about
understanding who you are, about feeling out what you do like
and exploring your options. I meet so many people who run businesses that they didn't traditionally train for, or would even have
thought of, but who were led down that path by opportunities
and their own curiosity.

If you are through and through a true businessperson—an entrepreneur—you're likely to run several businesses in the end; I don't think you'll have just one. Your business is going to change as you keep growing and continue the journey of life. Right? If you own a successful online retail store—selling sneakers, for example—eventually you're probably going to scale to a brick-and-mortar store or expand your brand to offer clothing and life-style items for sale as well. Whether you built your brand and your first business with a surfboard shop or by selling vintage handbags, your business model is not always going to look exactly the same way it did when you started your business. I started my business by doing guest speaking, and now the business has grown to include this book, podcasts, and TV. This is not something I ever thought I was going to do. But if you just stay open to the opportunities that present themselves, you're going to continue to grow wherever your business journey takes you.

Do Lean In to What You Like

Entrepreneurs lean into things that they like, right? Taking the opportunity to focus on something you like is usually the first entry point. What do I like? I like fashion. Okay, I want to have my own retail store. Maybe you like making lemonade, so you're going to make lemonade.

People will ask what your purpose is. I think that's such a heavily loaded question, and a hard one to answer in the early stages of your entrepreneurial endeavors. Instead, ask yourself what your passions are. Then sit down and really think about whether you're ready to be an entrepreneur. It's not an easy road, and the motivation to succeed and stick with it really has to come from you. No one else is going to do it for you. Lack of motivation is definitely the difference between businesses that do well and those that don't. When you think about your passion, remember that not everything has to be a business. If you pursue it as just a hobby, that's okay. Running a business is not for everyone.

Make a list of ten things that you like. What makes you happy? What lights you up? Maybe you'll realize that one of the things on your list could be turned into a hustle, a side hustle, or a full-on business.

Here, for example, are ten random things that I like:

1. Finances

2. Sharing my knowledge

3. Meditating

4. Studying the stock market

5. Investing

6. Travel

7. Dogs

8. Teaching kids

9. Studying art

10. Renovations

Do Have "Thick Skin"

Your business is your baby. You're going to need to be dedicated to it. No one is going to run your business for you; no one else will make success happen for you. And along the way, you're going to be told no. This is the same energy coming at you when you're trying to find a job, when you're going to be told no so many times.

I hate when people say, "You have to have 'thick skin,'" but in business, you really do have to have thick skin. You must be okay with hearing no. But remember, not all feedback is great feedback. Tell yourself: "You know what? Despite getting this no, I'm going to continue forward. I'm going to keep pushing. This is ultimately something that I want." So take to heart whatever feedback serves you and take everything else with a grain of salt. Because one day you'll look back and smile even wider when you hear that yes.

Do Stay Self-Motivated

I think the most important part of being an entrepreneur is staying self-motivated. Having the security of a job and a salary, filling out the forty-hour-per-week timesheets, all that looks a little different from the life of an entrepreneur, who's going to have to work nights and weekends sometimes and be continuously and creatively figuring out again and again how to keep scaling their business.

Don't Forget Self-Care

I cannot emphasize enough the importance of self-care. I know that when you're the one on the line, the one who has to make a business work, it's hard to make time for self-care. But if you burn out, there's no one else who's going to pick up those pieces. Take time to step away from your laptop, to step away from your business.

Especially when you're younger, you're in this mindset—hustle, hustle, hustle, hustle, hustle. You don't think about just enjoying your family and having quiet moments and downtime. But those things are important. Also, I think sometimes some of the biggest growth comes from not being so fixated on making something happen, but from just laughing and enjoying your life.

Don't Give Up If You Fail the First Time

If your business fails, that does not mean that you aren't good with finances. It also doesn't mean that you're not good at business. Don't give up. Even some of the greatest businesspeople sometimes experience the ebb and flow of business. For example Steve Jobs, the late CEO of Apple, had a few setbacks. In 1985, he started a business called NeXT, which provided computer workstations for educators. The business didn't work out, and he ran through millions of investment dollars. Then Apple bought that failing business from Jobs and rehired him in 1996.

So it's important to know that even the people you look up to, in spite of their great career and financial success, have had businesses fail or close or come dangerously close to failing before they saw that success. It really is about trial and error, but I don't want you to believe, if and when you go through it, that failure means you're not meant to be an entrepreneur. Your business may fail the first time, but if you don't keep trying and learning, you'll never see that success.

Do Use Your FU Fund

If you're interested in really getting something off the ground, build up your savings—your FU fund. Have money on the side in personal savings to use eventually as part of your startup funding, to cover the basics while you're getting your business off the ground. Sara Blakely, founder and CEO of Spanx, started her company with $5,000, and now it's worth billions. I'm a little bit more conservative, so I don't deplete my own savings account. Would I take a large portion out of it for a business I truly believed in? Yeah, but because I never want to see a zero balance anywhere, I'm more likely to leave some money in there for a rainy day as well.

Know, going in, that starting a business can sometimes be scary. But if using your own personal investment from your FU fund or from money put in by friends and family, you can go from there to find different loans and investors to help you scale and grow your business. You might have to deplete your savings to start your business, but again, as with investing, it is a high-risk, high-reward venture. Many people have done it, so don't be discouraged. If you believe your business is going to do fine, then take that on.

–12–

Money and Dating

When it comes to dating and money, I'm going to give it to you with love, but like it is, because sometimes we must hear the hard truth. I have a no-BS policy. I know who I am, I know what my money habits are, I know what I'm working toward, and I'm not going to let external factors change me in any way. That's how I approach investing, and that's how I approach dating and money and everything else. *The clearer you are about your identity, your needs, and your goals, the better equipped you can be in all aspects of your life, from dating to investing.*

What are you willing to compromise on when it comes to a romantic partner and money? What is an absolute deal-breaker?

When you're clear on your identity, needs, and goals, you can be more confident about dating. Here are a few other tips that might be useful to you.

Create a Dating Wish List

It may be smart to get clear about who you're trying to date and what you absolutely will not tolerate. The idea is to be clear but of course also open and flexible, to a point that still feels good to you. Be honest with yourself from the start, and then don't settle for less.

Know Your Deal-Breakers

Earlier in my twenties, I broke up with this gorgeous white guy despite whatever feelings I may have had for him at the time because he just did not make enough money or manage what he had well. He was also living in a sprawling apartment that was subsidized housing and so he was only paying $450 a month, which is a steal for what he had. Housing is where most people's paycheck goes. He was only spending $450 a month on housing in New York City and allegedly making six figures a year, and he didn't have a car or other expenses or a savings account, so then that made me question where all his money was going. This was a red flag for me. He was also six years older than me. One day I was in his room, and he had a bank statement out that said he had a $67,000 balance on a credit card. I almost passed out. His response to me was, "You're really going to break up with me because I don't make enough money? You don't know me, give me five years. I'll make enough money." My response was, "Maybe, maybe not. But if in five years you're making a lot of money, hit me back up."

This may seem harsh, but I come from a family where finances were a struggle. So, you see, this is an issue that specifically stresses me out. Not getting a good night's sleep because I'm stressed over someone else's finances, boyfriend or not, was a no-brainer. Especially because I have worked hard to not have any debt myself. One day I'm going to have to take care of my brother, to be financially responsible for my family, and I cannot have any added layers of financial stress. Ring my bell. If it's meant to be, it'll be. But that time the $67,000 debt was a deal-breaker.

Look, there are financial mistakes that people can fix, but fixing some mistakes or financial misfortunes can take a long time, and in the end some mistakes may prove not so easy to fix. I'm not alone in thinking this. In 2022, CNBC reported that 54 percent of people believe that debt is a reason to consider divorce. *Financial issues can spill over into your relationship.* For example, I read once that 38 percent of couples miss out on date nights because of debt.

I do want to say that having debt doesn't make you a bad person. And it doesn't mean that you don't deserve love in your life. We know that not all debt is bad, that debt can be your friend when you have a plan and you have decent income and a budget to manage it properly. It's possible to take on debt intentionally and with financial literacy and remain financially well. *But if you don't have a good relationship with money, then this is an issue I need to know about early on in a relationship.* That way I get to choose to date you or not, based on my own wants, needs, identity, and goals.

Some women are okay with being the main breadwinner, and I have met a lot of highly empowered women who are with a man who doesn't make as much money as they do or who has debt. There are women who are perfectly okay with that. But that's just not going to be me. Are you going to be okay with having a partner who doesn't make much money or who carries a lot of debt? Or is that not an issue for you?

If you're carrying a lot of debt yourself, you must understand what that actually means, what the truth of it is after taking off the rose-colored glasses. For example, say your partner has $400,000 in debt, and she's only making $30,000 a year. The reality is that she probably will never pay off that debt without significantly raising her income.

Ask yourself: "What does my partner's debt actually mean for the future of our relationship? Can I look past it? Past having that amount of debt constantly in our household budget?"

What if your partner lies about their debt? What if because of her spending habits, every paycheck goes to items purchased by credit card and kept hiding in the back of the closet? At what point is this behavior a problem? Are you going to be okay with this? Are you going to choose to love someone in spite of not only their emotional flaws but their financial flaws as well?

Some people might say: "I love this person despite their flaws, and I will continue to date them, and we'll just work on it together on a day-by-day basis." That's beautiful. But that's only possible when a partner is willing to learn and wants to do better. By creating a plan to raise their credit score, adopting better spending habits, and being more ambitious and setting goals. In this case, financial flaws can absolutely be fixed. But people make some mistakes early on that are more serious and have long-term consequences.

Another choice people make is looking at their relationship through rose-colored glasses thinking that the situation will change. But sometimes the other person doesn't even have the intention of changing. You may want more for this person than they want for themselves. They may be comfortable making a smaller salary of $20,000 a year. They may have no more ambition than that. But if you want more and don't get more, then you'll end up bumping heads with each other.

Communication Is Key

If your goal is to one day be wealthy and your partner's ambition is not at the same level as yours, is that going to work? Open the line of communication and find out. I just feel like that conversation doesn't happen enough. *To better identify true compatibility, it's important to know what the person you're dating thinks about money.*

You don't have to be tacky about it. You don't have to just start firing off questions, saying things like, "Let's talk about credit scores," and like, "Let's talk about debt." These are potentially touchy subjects for many people who are just uncomfortable talking about money, so do keep that in mind.

Start the Conversation Early

I think it's important to start talking about money early on, but I know couples who never talk about finances, never ever. Nine out of ten of them end up breaking up or ending their marriage after only a few years. And I'm not making this up—this percentage is supported by data. A survey of over two thousand adults by SunTrust Bank found that 35 percent of people named finances as the primary trouble spot with their partner. And research from the Federal Reserve showed that the greater the mismatch between a couple's credit scores, the more likely they were to break up within the first five years.

I always say that you must be willing to talk about money. Like, two months into dating someone, you can have that conversation. The sooner you express your intentions and financial needs when it comes to romance, the better off you'll be. Then there are no secrets between the two of you. You can be real, especially before things get too serious. How many figures do you aspire to earn? What tax bracket do you want to be in? Do you want children? A pet? A house? Would you be willing to relocate for a job? Are you willing to be the sole earner in your relationship? How much of the bills do you expect to pay? All, half, or only some?

Get Comfortable Asking Questions

I think you can have open conversations with the person you're dating without being tacky. You don't necessarily have to initiate that conversation on the second date, and you don't want to just blurt out, "So how much money do you make a year?" There are just so many more tactful ways to do that. But you can see if someone is financially responsible by asking the right questions. There is information you can gather about someone's financial picture without being too awkward or too blunt. You don't want to just come out and say: "What's your credit score and how much money do you make?"

I remember once having money conversations on the second date. During the conversation I asked, "What are your long-term financial goals?" and "What do you invest in?" I even asked about his credit score, which was funny because he wasn't from America, so he didn't really have a credit score. I ended up being the reason he wanted to figure out what his creditworthiness was here in America, and we laughed about that in a good way.

Financial Conversation Starters

▸ Do you keep up with your credit score?

▸ How do you put money toward savings?

▸ What are your financial goals for the future?

▸ Did you ever get into investing?

▸ Where do you live? Did you buy your home?

▸ Do you have a hobby? Do you collect things?

Who Picks Up the Check?

I'm old school. While I'm financially independent, I date men who don't mind paying for dinner. Obviously this is an old-fashioned perspective, to expect the man to pay for everything, but it's my personal preference. I'm not saying it's right or wrong, it's just what I like. I know that some people choose to go Dutch, and I even have had girlfriends who pay for everything. I think you should be up front and have an open conversation early on to define what your expectations are. Are you okay with paying for everything, or do you expect to split the check?

It may not seem that important at first, but you still need to express your expectations early on. *One of the number one reasons people break up is lack of communication about finances.* So if you're not making your expectations known early and truthfully, you can, and probably will, get disappointed down the road. Don't say that you're okay with paying for something when you're not.

When I am on a date, I will not even *pretend* to pull out my wallet. Some women will do that to test the waters—you know, like, *will he pay?* I'm not even going to set that expectation. But I will always say "thank you." I'm very Southern. I've been called out by gentlemen telling me that I don't have to say "thank you" after every date. But that is something that I need to do. I feel like it's only right: you're paying for dinner, so I'm going to say "thank you." That's just me.

You Can Date Tastefully and Within Your Budget

I remember this TikTok trend of people calling things like "oh, let's go for a walk" a "date." That's *not* a date! Walking? Going for a walk would feel like I'm hanging out with my friends, not going on a date.

Dates don't have to be expensive: you can go to the amusement park or the arcade, you can go to the movies, you can go to a carnival, you can go rock climbing. There are different things that you can do. Especially after I moved to LA, I heard people saying, "Let's go walk the beach." I'm like, *So, are we like getting ice cream? Or dinner? What are we doing besides walking? Because if I wanted to walk, I'm going to walk with my dog. I'm not going to get dressed up to go walking.*

Make an effort. A date is not a walk. A date is not Netflix and chill. Again, it's about setting expectations.

Set Boundaries

You can politely set boundaries to protect both your budget and your interests. If you let your date pick the restaurant, and they pick a five-money-sign ($$$$$) restaurant, then you need to be honest. If that doesn't fit into your weekend spending budget, or if you just don't feel like a date with this person is worth spending that much, it's perfectly fine to say, "Let me give you additional options." There are ways to do that without being demeaning or too vulnerable. Especially on a first date or the first few dates, just say, "Hey, how about these options?" If the response is like,

"No, I want more," maybe that's not the person you should be dating. It depends on how far you want to stretch your own expectations.

I look at my grandparents' love story as one example. My grandpa always overextended himself, and he probably does so even to this day, but he wants to make sure that he gives the best to his wife. That is what he wants to do, and they've been married for over fifty years. Whatever you extend yourself to do, understand that it's your choice to do it and don't feel bad or guilty or angry afterward, especially if you're spending intentionally and within your budget.

Own It!

Whatever the expectations you set, be intentional and own them. Don't be delusional. Sometimes relationships are transactional. Yeah, I mean that, and yes, I said that. And listen, I was raised to be independent, and not to get all glossy-eyed over someone dangling a luxury handbag or someone saying, "I'll fly you out." Live your own life, you only live once. That said, if you want the handbag, take the handbag, but know that offering it to you means that they probably want to have sex with you. If you want that free trip to Vegas, then go for it. But know what that trip to Vegas means and own it. Do what you do and own it authentically. Feel good about the decisions you make.

I've never accepted trips, but more power to the people who go on those trips, or who get their college paid for. Good for you doing that. You may get your rent paid. And I'm saying this without judgment because I'm all about people just being authentically truthful about what their intentions are. The same goes for the person doing the spending. You have to know what your intentions are. Know what the agreement is going in. Know if this relationship is just for now, know if the other person is likely to take your gifts, and know that when they're ready they might bounce. When that happens, it's all just been transactional. Know if you want more than just a transactional relationship and then don't settle for less.

Common Financial Dating Don'ts

▸ Do not screw up your finances when you're dating for love. A lot of people do this!

▸ Don't get a car for someone.

▸ Don't invite the person you're dating to share your bank account.

▸ Don't put that person on your credit card.

▸ Don't move in together without having an open conversation about expectations.

▸ Don't cash checks for your partner; you could get mixed up in fraud.

▸ Don't deposit large amounts of cash into your bank account for someone you hardly know.

▸ Don't have a joint bank account.

▸ Don't spend outside of your budget or on credit just to try to impress someone.

Dating Red Flags

▸ The person you're dating avoids talking about money.

▸ Your date dresses flashy but can't explain what they do for a living. How can they afford their clothes and jewelry?

▸ The person you're dating is always open and available.

▸ This person asks to use your credit card.

▸ The person you're dating is always leaving their wallet at home, or their Cash App/Venmo doesn't work.

▸ Someone you're really into asks to deposit large amounts of cash into your bank account. I know someone this happened to. She met someone she really liked through an online dating site. Allegedly this person made a lot of money. One day he said: "Oh, by the way, can I transfer $200,000 to your bank account?" The answer here is "Absolutely not!"

▸ Don't be blind to financial scams because you think you really like the person. Unfortunately, so many have been conned by people who are con artists and who take advantage of their partners. We read these stories online and hear about them in documentaries. It's important to take off those rose-colored glasses and be smarter than that. Remember, if it seems too good to be true, it probably is.

▸ You're always paying for everything. The person you're dating doesn't have a job and doesn't seem to be looking for one either. This is just going to get worse. If someone is taking advantage of you now, they'll probably do the same in the future.

▸ The person you're dating is readily available to move in immediately.

Be Intentional!

You're worth it. If a relationship no longer works for you or just doesn't feel good anymore, know that you have the power to change your mind, your circumstances, and your romantic life. Don't settle to please other people. Carry that same energy into jobs, relationships, and your career. When you want the best for yourself, when you want more, that's when you open yourself up to the possibilities out there for you to experience happiness, success, and wellness.

−13−

Giving

Every day, in my stillness, I think about the act of giving. I write about it in my journal or even say it out loud. I make it a habit to thank people I've met and those who have helped me along the way. I pray that their dreams come true. I may say a small affirmation, putting it out there that they will have an amazing day. Sometimes I may tip a little extra at restaurants. In a drive-thru line, sometimes I pay for the car behind me. I do small things without asking for anything in return.

The moment I started these small acts of giving, I felt everything that I was trying to manifest come true. Giving put me vibrationally in a more energetic and happy place. Giving can leave you feeling good, and it can brighten the day of others. When you want people to feel good, aligning yourself with the energy of giving and receiving is transformational. You may find that the job will come, the money will come, and you'll keep it and grow your wealth, and the more wealth you grow, the more empowered you will be to continue in this energy.

Many people think that those who pursue money are shallow, materialistic, self-centered, or opportunistic. But money does make the world go round. When we empower ourselves with financial wellness, we can more easily be in a place to support the charities and institutions and causes that light us up. We can be in a better position to empower the dreams and goals of ourselves and others. We can change the direction of someone's life in a positive way that may be generational.

For me, it has never been about the superficial aspects of money, about being able to say, "I wear this designer," or, "I carry this card." My journey has become about sharing information that can empower those who have too often been left out of the conversation. For too long, for example, men have been more comfortable than women talking about money and managing and saving for retirement. It isn't a coincidence that there were more men working with me in finance than women, as well as more white men than Black and brown people.

Giving is important to me, and there are so many ways to do it. Giving is not always about money, and I wanted to stress that. That's what lights up my heart, what drives me to do what I do.

You can, of course, give your money, but there are many ways to give beyond monetary donations:

‣ You can give your time.

‣ You can share your knowledge or wisdom.

‣ You can give a smile.

‣ You can give a compliment.

‣ You can say hello to people who are normally unseen, like people experiencing homelessness.

‣ You can give a student an internship.

‣ You can write a recommendation for a student or job-seeker.

‣ You can teach a class.

‣ You can give career advice.

‣ You can pass a résumé on to someone you know in HR.

‣ You can cook a meal or bake a cake for someone.

‣ You can call someone to check in and see if they're doing okay.

‣ You can listen, without judgment, to someone who needs to talk.

‣ You can send prayers and blessings to others.

‣ You can register your dog as a "therapy" dog and take it to volunteer with you at schools, hospitals, or nursing homes.

I want you to never feel obligated to give to organizations or to people who have not been supportive or who do not align with your values.

As I was working on this chapter, my team happened to get a call from my alma mater. Every single year for the past four years they've invited me to come back and speak to the students. And every year my team lets them know that I have a speaking fee. I'm a professional speaker, and this is one of the ways I make my money. And every year my fee goes up because I work hard at being the best speaker I can be.

As my team negotiated back and forth, the school continually dropped the name of another speaker they had been able to engage. This speaker was a white man who apparently is successful in his career and has written a ton of books and screenplays for very famous celebrities. That's wonderful, and I was happy for this person's career success. But I didn't understand what his career success had to do with the negotiations with me.

What the school seemed to be trying to do—and you may find this happening at some point in your own career—was to devalue my expertise. Mentioning another speaker and how wonderful they were was a passive-aggressive way to compare me with a speaker whose accomplishments and accolades they apparently valued more.

They finally made their pitch: "Anyways, we would love for you to come speak to students."

"Well then," I said, "we will have to work around my schedule. Black History Month could be a great time for me to speak."

And they responded, "Great, because we have openings in January and March."

I was in shock. Not only were they asking a professional African American woman speaker to appear at the school for free, not only did they attempt to devalue my time by comparing me to a white male speaker they'd obtained, but they also had no idea that Black History Month happens in February. I was even more shocked to learn that my team and I had been on the phone with the dean.

What does this have to do with giving? Giving is something that you should never feel obligated to do. Give because you feel it. Because you want to give. And you especially shouldn't feel obligated to give to people and institutions who have given you little in return. Who have not supported you in your dreams.

My alma mater, for example, didn't get me a job or offer me a powerful alumni network, and it never gave me a scholarship, career counseling, or access to a mentor. Now that I'm in a strong place in my career, it benefits them if I speak to their students, but they still asked me to do it for free. And while I do speak for free when I'm feeling it, I'm careful not to give my time and my talents to organizations that don't make the giving a mutually beneficial exchange.

One school that I will always go back to when I can is KIPP. I went to a KIPP charter school, TEAM academy, for one year in middle school. I will forever be grateful to them and grateful that they give not just me, but all students, some level of support.

With the little bit of funds they had, they also gave stipends each semester to students after they entered college. When I graduated from college, they set up interviews for me at top-tier companies. They provided me with mental support and invested in me all around. They even provided an executive coach for me. That's not to say I don't have criticisms of KIPP organizations, but they were helpful to me and my career development.

Giving Back Shouldn't Feel Like an Obligation

When Christmas and other holidays toward the end of the year come around, people feel like, "I need to give back." No. *Give back where you want to give back, not where you feel obligated to do it.* You may not be at the point in your life where you *can* give back, and that is okay. Sometimes, financially, we're not in a place to give, and sometimes, spiritually, we're not in a place to give.

But when you are in that place, when you have absolutely no excuses to *not* give, then give back. That is the ultimate, altruistic goal. That is what we should be striving for. I think sometimes people feel like, "Oh, she's Black, she needs to be doing this," or,

"Oh, he's a man, he needs to be doing this." Oh, and the list goes on—you can fill in the blanks. Sometimes people just aren't at a place to give back, financially or otherwise.

Give back in a space where you want to give back.
Giving shouldn't feel like an obligation.

Sometimes it may look like people are in a place to help, but that's just not always the truth of the matter. Sometimes people are not in the place to make the connections for you, or to give you the referral, because they're busy building themselves up. They can't help you. I recently heard Gina Prince-Bythewood, the director of *The Woman King*, during an Instagram Live session with Black Girls Rock say that back when she was just starting out she approached John Singleton for help with her script and she got a similar answer. He liked her script, but he couldn't help. He was busy trying to get his own career in a good place. This happens, and we can't take it personally. We never know what prevents someone from giving.

While I didn't grow up in the church, my grandparents are very much rooted in the church, and so they have a giving mind-set. They like to give their time. That mindset is positive in certain aspects. But I'm not for giving if you're not truly wanting to give. Vibrationally, your giving should be in the right place. *Look for*

199

organizations that light you up and energize you, that make you want *to give.*

Sometimes You Can Give Without Expectations

Should I expect something back in return? Although that's a question I sometimes struggle with, I have come to realize that the ultimate charity and gift giving happens when you really don't want anything in return. This kind of off-the-books giving works for personal charity in instances where, for example, you give in the street to a person who asks for help and looks like they may really need it, and being able to do that will energize you.

When Giving to Institutions, You Should Expect Something in Return

When I give to an organization, I do want it to give something back to me. I expect to see results from that organization. When you give to an organization, ask yourself these questions:

What does the organization do for the community that makes you excited?

What does it do for the people around you?

Does this organization give out free meals to the public?

Does this organization help those living with cerebral palsy?

Does it help homeless or injured pets?

Does it help the elderly?

What work has this organization done in the past?

What is it in this organization's mission that energizes me?

Look for causes, charities, and organizations that make you say, "I want to be a part of this."

Give to organizations that you can feel good about, that make you feel like your dollar, or your volunteer time, will really make a difference. Ultimately that's what it boils down to, that's the goal.

When it's right, you can feel it in your gut, in the same way that you feel like you can manifest making a million dollars, in the same way you feel like you can move up in your career. That is the energy you want to feel when you're choosing a cause, a mission, or a charity. No one can muster up those feelings for you. It really should be something that comes from you. But I do believe that once you feel this energy, it's a very powerful experience.

Again, you have to feel it and you have to want to give back; you have to want to empower others. When I first started on the trading floor, I never really felt like I had an obligation as a Black woman to give back. But I was called by my gut to want

201

to teach people, to pass along this information that I have. Once that clicked for me, I knew that that this was something that I wanted to do. Giving back from my experience is now one of my passions, part of my purpose, and I've sought out ways to give back in this way.

The Difference Between Donating Out of Obligation and Donating Because You Truly Care

I've been at the charity events. I've sat at the table where all of these people were writing $100,000 checks. At the time, I had just come fresh off of the trading floor and didn't have money to write a check to charity of that size. But that's when I began to notice that certain people get involved in charity in a specific way, and at specific times. I noticed the charitable donations, especially the huge ones, flowing around the holidays. And that's when I came to understand that there is a difference between donating to charity or a cause because you feel obligated to and donating because you really want to.

When I sat in those rooms watching billionaires write these $100,000 checks to, for example, Black and brown students, I saw that there is a big difference between donating and *donating*. These billionaires were donating out of a sense of obligation, because it made them look good, and because it was the end of the year and they were thinking about the tax write-off. They were not donating because they really wanted to see someone achieve and move forward with some financial help from them.

There are definitely benefits to writing off donations on your taxes, but are you really donating with good intentions? Or are you doing it just to do it? I think those are two different ways that you can donate.

I wish more people who make donations would ask themselves:

▸ How do you manifest the spirit of your donation within your own organization?

▸ After you give to an organization, are you actually following up with the progress it's making?

▸ Are you going to reach out to the beneficiaries of your donation afterward?

I've seen the answer straight up: No. You're not really interested. You're just taking a picture with the kids because it looks good for you.

I was kind of taken aback to learn after I met one of the high-powered executives of color in my industry that he was very comfortable sitting at the charity table and giving in a public setting but privately wasn't practicing diversity of hiring. He was in the position to hire, to give back through internships and to give back through jobs. When I asked him how many people of color worked in his organization, he mentioned four: himself at the top, a receptionist, an assistant, and a custodial worker. He didn't seem to think that there was anything at all wrong with this. I am not in the position to question his intentions, but actions do speak volumes. His answer to my question made me wonder whether, as a Black man, he was giving that night only out of obligation.

On the other hand, I have met people who are truly authentic about their giving, and you can see this giving mindset in all areas of their organization. They may practice diversity of hiring or regularly reach out to offer *paid* internships to kids in the community or give year-round as part of their corporate or organizational structure. Beyond holiday giving, how are you showing up for the community around you?

Don't Feel Pressured into Giving Right Away

When people or organizations approach you to give, you don't have to feel rushed to give right there and then. You can ask a lot of questions, request their website information or QR code, and then do your research and figure out if it's something worth giving to.

I was at the grocery store when people from DARE were set

up outside. DARE, founded by the Los Angeles Police Department and the Los Angeles Unified School District, has been around for a while now. I kind of laughed when I was reminded of its motto: "Don't do drugs." I've never personally known anyone to go through the DARE program and turn away drugs. People do what they do, right? I did, however, end up donating after I asked this question: "What else are you doing outside of telling people to not do drugs?" They responded, "We build homes for the homeless and provide meals for them." That lit me up.

Remember that there are alternative ways to support charitable efforts and good causes that appeal to you. Always be asking: "What else can I do? How else can I support this work?"

Practice Charity by Sending Positive Vibes

Sometimes I go through every interaction that I've had throughout the day, just thinking about the people I've met that day, and I send these people blessings. I wish them a good day, a good life, the best in their career. I say: "Thank you for this interaction." *Sending positive vibes to others is a form of giving.*

The other day, while I was house-hunting, I met this adorable little girl in an adorable dress made of this cute watermelon print. Her energy just lit me up, and I wrote about her in my journal.

I wrote that I was just so grateful for the interaction, for that little moment when she came over to say hi and smiled and talked to me. I had that little two-to-five-minute moment with her, and it warmed my heart. So later that day I took some time to just wish the best for this little girl in her life, as well as for her family; I wished that their house-hunting journey would be beautiful and that everything would work out for them exactly the way it was meant to.

Don't Put a Figure on How Much to Give

If you are entitled and you want to give the entire amount of your budget to charity, then go for it. I look at the billionaires, such as Bill Gates, who have pledged to give most of their wealth to charity through the Giving Pledge, an initiative set up by America's wealthiest in August 2010. Giving is personal: whether you want to give the majority of your wealth or just a dollar, if you truly feel good about that then go for it. I want people to never feel like they have to give out of obligation. Everyone's financial situation and capacity to give is different.

Also, don't ever give and give and give to your own detriment. If you don't have enough to give, you should probably focus on giving to your savings and emergency funds instead. Give later down the line when you're in a better financial position.

Know the Current Tax Laws and Limitations on Giving

When you give to qualifying charities, your giving can be tax-deductible. You'll want to check with the IRS or your accountant to make sure that, for that tax year, the organization, monetary amount, form of giving, and timing of your gift qualify for tax deductions. Not all giving qualifies. Usually donations to political organizations, nonprofits, religious organizations, civil defense organizations, fraternities and sororities, educational and scientific institutions, and organizations dedicated to the prevention of cruelty to children and animals that are registered as 501(c)(3) organizations will qualify as tax-deductible under IRS code 170.

If you're going to give large amounts of money to a person who is not your spouse or an organization, know that you may need to pay a gift tax on the amount you give. The person giving the gift is often the one responsible for paying the gift tax. Most gifts given to individuals, but not to charities, are taxed. There are some exceptions to this rule, including gifts below the annual limit, gifts given to a spouse, tuition, medical expenses that you pay for someone, and gifts to political organizations. It can get tricky, so when you're giving away large sums of money to individuals, be sure to know the rules about how much you can give and what percentage of your salary you can give away. Also be aware that these rules can change from year to year.

For the tax year 2021, for example, you could give away 100 percent of your salary and get a tax deduction if you itemized. If you didn't itemize, you could get a tax deduction on up to only $300 in cash donations to charities as an individual and $600 in tax-deductible donations as a married couple. This rule may change for the 2023 tax year and beyond. Check irs.gov for current information on tax-deductible giving.

Give from Your Heart

When I was growing up, I once woke up in the middle of the night and saw red and orange everywhere. I thought a house had to be on fire, but I didn't smell smoke. But then I looked out the window and realized that the house across the street was on fire. Without even thinking twice, my family came out to help. We brought our neighbors blankets, sheets, and towels. They were brand-new; we'd literally just bought them, and some still had the tags on. It wasn't anything that we even paused to think about; it was just the least that we could do to help our neighbors. We never saw them again after that night, but we do know that they're doing okay. We feel thankful that we were able to help in some way. That kind of giving—to people in immediate need, without expecting anything in return—can really light you up. You'd hope that people would do the same for you.

It's all about being in the mindset where you really want to empower, you really want to give, you really want to invest in doing those things. If you don't, then that's also okay. No one should judge you; no one should tell you that you *have* to empower people. You have to *want* to empower people, and wanting to empower people is going to come down to the individual person. It is really altruistic to say, "Yeah, empower, give back, do this, do that." If you don't want to, though, you don't have to. I'm not here to judge you.

But once it clicks for you, that desire to give back, it can be life-changing. The moment I started giving back I started seeing instrumental changes in my career and my success and in how I've grown and maneuvered.

Financial Terms You Should Know

I know that I've been mentioning a ton of financial words in this book. You'll also find that I mention these terms during my podcasts, on CNBC, in my Instagram stories, when speaking on TV, and while consulting. I recently found myself sitting with a few clients who happened to be very successful and talented people in their field. They were at the top of the game, yet it began to dawn on me, as I threw around some common financial terms, such as "inflation" and "asset classes," that my clients weren't always following along. When I used the term "portfolio," one of my clients stopped me for a moment to ask if by portfolio I meant an actual book. I was more than happy for the honest question and thrilled to give the answer.

No matter how successful you are, how many millions you have, how on top of your game you are, how many championships you've won, how many awards you may have in your field, know that no one person can possibly know everything about everything. Each of us is an expert in what we love, eat, sleep, and breathe. For me that's finance. People have a million questions for me whenever I'm speaking, and I love that. Education is a huge part of why I do my job. Helping people understand finance is part of my job as a consultant. People may just not have the time to learn these things, especially when they're out making millions. That's why they hire me—for the financial expertise I've developed after years of experience on the floor of the Exchange as well as just in life.

I love when people I meet along the way have the confidence to ask questions, to admit that they don't know. I love when people truly want to learn and have gotten to a place where they're open to asking questions about money and are no longer afraid to face their finances, to check their bank account, to make a budget. That eagerness to learn just energizes me.

When my client asked me what "portfolio" means I was re- minded of the intention I held in my heart when I set out to write this book. The truth is that so many of us don't grow up knowing common financial terms, unless it's our field of choice, or we got curious and started studying on our own, or we had parents or someone around who taught us. That's not the case for most people. And that's okay. I am proud that you picked up this book, that maybe you have tuned into my podcasts or watch Bloomberg or CNBC or some other source for financial news. Every little bit is progress toward your own financial empowerment and sets your future on an empowered path to the resources you need to manifest your dreams and goals.

When it comes to money and finances, there's always so much to learn, and the more you learn, the more you realize that there's always something new to learn. Just when maybe we felt we knew everything, along came NFTs in October 2015, and then Bitcoin, the first cryptocurrency, in 2019. These were completely new financial entities that we needed to research and try to wrap our minds around if we were to keep on making the best choices for our financial goals. We had to decide if we were going to follow that trend or sit this one out and wait to see what happened. I never trusted crypto, but I commend everyone who did their own research and took their chances; some of them did well, and others did not. Sometimes it's not about whether you win or lose, it's more about what you learn along the way. A lot of finance is about taking informed chances. That's why it's really important to set clear goals.

I'm really big on people having an expansion mindset. That's a wealth mindset. If you watch the most successful people, you'll see that they're always learning new things and staying open to new knowledge. We have to keep learning. Wealthy folks keep learning. People who stay humble and continue to expand their knowledge are the people who will master financial wellness and literacy and master the principles in this book. They're the ones who will one day understand almost every term that their financial adviser, bank, credit card company, or car dealership throws their way or presents in the fine print. Understanding common financial terms gives you power, for instance, to understand if that mortgage is going to work best for you.

Again, it's perfectly okay if you're hearing the terms mentioned in this book for the first time. Many of us never took economics in school, some of our parents never talked to us about money, and finance just wasn't part of our lives growing up. Still, it's important to understand what common financial words mean. Don't feel bad if they don't seem to make sense to you at first. Just keep tuning in to that podcast or watching that business news. Eventually you will find that it does start to make sense.

And don't forget: Google is your best friend. If you don't know it or can't remember it, look it up! The more you read and keep a mindset of being open to learning, the better off you'll be when it comes to learning and using financial terms.

Here are a few common financial terms that you should know. Practice saying them to yourself in the mirror. They'll look good on you!

Asset

An item that has value and is owned by a person, a business, or a financial entity. A *liquid* asset can be easily and quickly turned into cash. An *intangible* asset is a valuable but nonphysical entity. For example, intellectual property, such as a trademark and patent, is considered an intangible asset.

Asset classes

The many different categories of investments and valuables owned by a person or company, such as stocks, bonds, gold, or real estate.

Balance sheet

A snapshot of the financial health of a company; it includes their assets and liabilities. Assets are what they own and liabilities are what they owe.

Bank

A financial institution that accepts deposits into checking and savings accounts in which you can store your money. You can write checks from a checking account, but not from a savings account. Banks also lend money to borrowers through loans and mortgages. Types of banks include FDIC-insured commercial banks, credit unions, investment banks, and online banks.

Bear market

During a bear market you'll see stock prices fall, you'll see job losses. A bear market typically foreshadows an economic downturn about six months to a year before it hits the greater economy as a recession or economic depression.

Budget

A financial plan to use as a guide to responsibly saving, investing, and spending your money.

Bull market

A period when the economy is thriving. You'll typically see stock markets and different asset classes rising.

Capital gains

The profit you make on an investment when you sell an asset for more than what you paid for it.

Credit

A legal agreement between a person or entity that lends money and a borrower who is understood to be obligated to pay that money back at a later date, and most likely with interest.

Credit score

A score given to a borrower by a credit-issuing agency, a third-party entity that is not a bank or government agency. A credit score is based on a borrower's credit history. Demonstrating that you can use credit responsibly and strategically will earn you a good credit score.

Equity

Partial ownership of a company or an asset. For instance, you can have equity in a home.

Finance

All things related to the study, creation, and management of money and all things related to money.

Financial adviser

A professional who provides financial advice and financial planning services to clients and customers in exchange for a fee.

Generational wealth

Wealth that is passed down in the family from one generation to the next. For example, your grandmother leaves you a home and you pay to maintain it and keep it in the family.

Income

Money that a person or entity earns from their work, trade, skill, company revenues, or investments. Income can be paid in the form of a paycheck, cash, or a digital transfer. *Business income* is money that a business earns for selling goods and services. *Passive income* is money you receive without actively working for it—for example, through investments, which increase in value with no work effort on your part.

Inflation

What's happening when the value of your dollar buys less and
less. During an inflationary period, you will see the prices of
goods go up. When you hear someone say they could buy a slice
of pizza for a dollar when they were growing up but now it costs
three dollars, they're talking about inflation.

Interest

The money a borrower pays for the use of a lender's money,
usually a percentage of the initial amount borrowed. You can
also earn interest on assets you own, such as government bonds.

Investment

Money put into an asset with the intention of eventually making
even more money on it. The asset may gain in value slowly
over time or very quickly. Most investments have risk and the
potential to lose money.

Liability

The opposite of an asset, it's money that a person or entity owes
to another. For example, credit card debt and student loans are
liabilities.

Loan

An amount of money that a lender lends to a borrower, who must
pay this money back within an agreed-upon length of time and

with an agreed-upon amount of interest and fees. Whether you're taking out a student loan, home loan, or car loan, you always want to pay attention to the fine print of the loan agreement.

Market index

The index used to keep track of the performance of a group of stocks, bonds, or other investments, which are usually sorted into categories and types of industries.

Mortgage

A loan taken out on a home, which is used as *collateral*. That means, if you don't pay your mortgage for a long enough period of time, the lender can take back your home.

Net worth

The total value of what a person or business owns (assets such as a home, jewelry, art, etc.) minus what they owe (liabilities such as credit cards, loans, and mortgages).

Portfolio

A portfolio is not a physical book! It's a collection of assets. Stocks, bonds, and mutual funds may all be a part of your portfolio.

Recession

A period of time when the economy isn't doing so well and trade, markets, and industry are all going through a slump.

Retirement
The age when a person leaves the workforce. In the United States the retirement age is sixty-five.

Securities
A certificate of ownership or a certificate of credit to the right to own assets like stocks, bonds, or derivatives.

Stock exchange
A market where securities are bought and sold.

Stock market
A market where equities, or shares of companies, are bought and sold.

Taxes
Fees paid by people, businesses, and other entities to the government that it uses to fund public services like fixing roads and bridges. The Internal Revenue Service (IRS) keeps track of taxes owed and paid in the United States. While there are a number of ways to get around paying your taxes, tax evasion is against the law.

Conclusion

I wrote this book for the others in the room. Did you know that households headed by white adults are more likely than those headed by Black or Hispanic adults to have investments in the stock market? According to a 2020 Pew Research study, 61 percent of white households own stock, but only 31 percent of Black households and 28 percent of Hispanic households do. I want readers of this book to know that financial wellness, financial literacy, and financial empowerment and freedom are achievable for everyone, not just for some.

Looking at Wall Street from the outside, you might feel like you need to have some higher advanced degree in economics or finance in order to play the game, and that's just not the truth. The principles behind finance are simple, based on processes and habits we have been practicing our entire lives. When you go to the store to buy chips, you're making a trade. If you borrow money from a friend, you're taking out a loan. Do you set aside certain amounts of money to spend only on groceries? You're making a budget.

Now that you know the basics of math, of trade, of concepts like lending, maybe even of betting on sports teams, you just need to put that practice into play. Putting the principles outlined in *Make Money Move* to work, you can now bet on or against stocks and securities, budget in hypermode, and form a grown-up, more advanced view of money management.

In finance, we have this rule: no one is allowed to say that something is "100 percent guaranteed." So I'm careful not to use absolutes. But I will say that if you apply what you've learned in this book and change your mindset, you could change the course of your financial future, and your children's future. If you practice what I have laid out in this book, take the time to understand the concepts, and try to learn even more, you will change your money habits and your entire relationship with money. You may also become a savvy money manager and a better investor.

Why are these financial practices important? Especially for the others in the room who didn't grow up knowing about them? Because we want to actually grow our money. We spend a lot of the money we earn, but not on assets, things that can grow our wealth. We need to spend our money in ways that will create generational wealth. That is the ultimate American dream. That's everyone's ultimate dream, not just Americans'—the dream of creating generational wealth. That hasn't been achievable for so many of us because we've been left out of the room, left in the dark. Or, if we have managed to create some wealth, we haven't taught our children the principles of money management, and maybe they lose it. Or maybe we built it but it was destroyed, taken from us, like in the Tulsa race riots. Or maybe we gained wealth, mismanaged it, and were left broke, like so many of the ballplayers and celebrities you read about.

Generational wealth provides financial stability, security, and hope for the future.

What does financial wellness look like? What does it feel like? What do you imagine your life will be when you're finally financially secure? We have touched on the fact in this book that money is one of the leading causes of stress, which leads to disease and so many health disparities. So keeping a *Make Money Move* mindset that protects you from worries about paying your bills and enables you to one day buy what you need, like a house, as you invest your money and watch it grow—it's an amazing feeling. *You just feel supported.* You feel like you're wrapped in a warm and comfortable blanket, like it will be okay.

It is an amazing day when you reach that level of financial fitness, when you know that everything will be okay. That feeling of just excelling beyond the financial worries, hardships, and anxieties of the past is indescribable. Knowing that everything is going to be just fine from a mental standpoint, from a body standpoint, and from a wealth standpoint—I want that for everyone. I want you to achieve that level of comfort and stability.

Look, I know what it's like when you don't have much. You're nervous. You're always worried, your heart is racing, and your palms are sweaty. You're always thinking in real time, the present, instead of thinking in the future. You're never having that moment to just feel a sense of relief. Instead, every moment is scary and stressful. You're super worried and paranoid, and you have that knot in your stomach. It's not a comfortable feeling whatsoever.

Through financial empowerment, I hope to alleviate that stress for you. When money is no longer a stress factor or problem in your world, then you can feel invincible. Like a superhero, you will feel like you can actually take on the world. You'll feel independent, like you don't have to rely on other people. You won't have to wait for others to give you an answer. You'll feel limitless.

That stress you feel when your money isn't right doesn't discriminate. I know people who have a high net worth and a lot of money but they still live paycheck to paycheck. So, again, it really is about creating that wealth mindset. Once you strike that balance where everything is interconnected, it's liberating. It means freedom. It means comfort. And this sense of freedom and comfort will speak in the way you walk, the way you talk, the way you glow, showing your level of confidence. You've just gotten to a very Zen place and aren't stressed anymore.

You wake up every day and look at the world differently.

Now that I am reaching an income of a million, I really do feel like I'm in that place and can take on the world. My outlook, my interests, and my learning are no longer all tied to money. I can actually worry about things that are impactful, if that makes sense. I have gotten to a place where my outlook has gone from survival and hustle to thinking of ways to give back. I wake up with questions not like, How am I going to pay my rent?, but like, How can I give back? How can I empower others like I have empowered myself? How can I get more people to feel this way?

This woman recently came up to me after one of my speeches and pulled me aside. She told me that she's in finance today because she heard my story. She explained that she came from the middle of America, the middle of nowhere, and grew up with little money. But hearing my story empowered her to go into finance. She said that I'd made her feel like she too could take on the world. And now she was making more money than ever. She thanked me for being that inspiration to her.

That wasn't the first time in my life when someone has come up to me and shared a story like that. But her story moved me to tears as I realized I could be that inspiring person for someone. Especially because, when I was growing up I was bullied frequently, often overlooked, and not taken seriously.

I want more people to feel like they can be that person, especially when it comes to money. Look, maybe it's not working in finance that can be what makes you feel empowered. But know that you can take on your finances. Know that you can just start, right now. And know that you will do just fine, regardless of your background, regardless of where you come from. I hope that the tools in this book can help you do that. Be intentional. You're limitless. You are absolutely limitless. This may sound cheesy, but the world is yours. The world is yours. Don't take no for an answer. Learn to pick your fights. Learn to know who your allies are, and lean into people who are actually going to uplift and support you. What's meant for you will be for you. Do not give up. You have to believe, dream, and then get to work.

You will be so surprised about where your mind can take you, but whether it's a dark place or a good place, your mind is what will unlock this world for you. So use your mind to help you get where you want to go and where you want to be. Five years from now you're going to look back at some of the affirmations you wrote in this book and you're just going to realize, yeah, I achieved some of these things that I created in my mind—and then some!

Acknowledgments

I would like to extend my deepest gratitude to my agent, Kate-lyn Dougherty, and the entire Paradigm team, including Alyssa Reuben. These deals never happen instantly, and there was a moment where I thought no one would be interested in wanting to publish or buy my book, and two years later, after my story went viral and pitch after pitch, I got three offers and cried because people did care. I want to thank the incredible people that I get to reach through my words even more.

IDA JOHN, it's crazy that I have known you since we were in middle school. I'm in awe of your talent and how you recognized my beauty especially in moments where I was made to feel small. You always make me look big and incredible, and I'm so grateful to have had a Black woman shoot this cover.

To my editor, Patrik Henry Bass, and to the entire team at HarperCollins, thanks for helping to bring my vision to life.

Glendon Palmer of AGC, you recognized that my story needed to be shared with the world on the big screen, and without you making a deal on my life rights, none of my other projects would have been lifted off the ground. You are a selfless person who is constantly connecting the dots for me and introducing me to incredible people who now make up my team. I am forever grateful for you being so genuine.

Imani Powell-Razat, thanks for being a brilliant writer who transforms my words to paper. The hours we sat and worked on this book. The tears, the laughter, the commonalities. I'm grateful to have had such an incredible person to help me with this book.

Thanks to Kim Yau of Echo Lake, my first agent, who encouraged me to write a book and introduced me to Katelyn and Alyssa.

For first sharing my story, Joe Miller at BBC; without that news article going viral there would never have been a book deal.

Courtney Connley for sharing my story in America and just encouraging me throughout this entire journey.

Max Cutler at Spotify for being a dear friend and saying no initially to my podcast but encouraging me to take on new projects and continuously validating what I have to offer to the world.

To KIPP NJ, for forever supporting my family and me, and for listening to shows and reading my book and being an extended family.

Thanks, Mom!

About the Author

Affectionately known as the "Wolfette of Wall Street," at twenty-two, Lauren Simmons made history, becoming the youngest trader on the NYSE floor, and only the second African American female trader to work on the Exchange in over 228 years. After earning her badge on the trading floor, Lauren has successfully grown her brand and is a global motivational speaker, author, producer, and host. Lauren's perspective is one of a kind. And because of her insights she has inspired and empowered countless women, minorities, millennials, and Gen Zers with regard to the world of finance and financial wellness. Living a financially wealthy life isn't just about making the money but is also about the holistic lifestyle that goes with it. It's about getting your mind right, your body right, and making your money move. She is a credible expert beyond social media. Lauren has no interest in just being viral on social media, and it shows because she transcends all media platforms. She is at the intersection of finance and entertainment and does so effortlessly.

Lauren is an advocate for the financial sector to take steps to increase diversity and inclusion. She has countless accolades, including being named "Woman of the Year" by *Harper's Bazaar*, recognized as a "Woman of Impact" by *Politico*, and named "Woman in Power" by *Black Enterprise* in 2023—despite being only twenty-eight years old. Kevin O'Leary, Michael Strahan, Gabrielle Union, and Drew Barrymore have sung Lauren's praises of her financial guidance being accurate, young, and fresh. And certainly she holds her own alongside incredible business women such as Barbara Corcoran.

As a broadcaster, Lauren inked two podcast deals with Spotify: *Mind Body Wealth*, which debuted at number two on the top business podcasts in the US, and *Money Moves*. Lauren is also partnered with BlackRock/NBA in a digital series helping young rookies as their financial coach. She empowers young investors to understand the importance of investing through one of her digital streaming series, *Invested*, with Robinhood and *Refinery29*. She graces the TV screen of GMA, CNBC, and *Business Insider* and so many more as a subject matter expert in finance, especially during this economic downturn. Furthermore, she sits on the boards of various publicly traded companies. She has a biopic, *Midas Touch*, coming out with AGC Studios starring Chloe Bailey and directed by Numa Perrier on which Lauren is an executive producer. And if that isn't enough, this book debuted on presale on Amazon as a number one new release as well as in the top one hundred books in the personal money management space. Lauren is not just strictly finance, as she has been the face for global campaigns with Express, LinkedIn, Ford, McDonald's, Pure Leaf, and Lady Champs. Through her various partnerships and her own personal social media, in the past year she has had well over fifty million impressions.